Past Masters
General Editor Keith Thomas

Augustine

For Juliet

Past Masters

AQUINAS Anthony Kenny
ARISTOTLE Jonathan Barnes
ARNOLD Stefan Collini
AUGUSTINE Henry Chadwick
BACH Denis Arnold
FRANCIS BACON Anthony
    Quinton
BAYLE Elisabeth Labrousse
BENTHAM John Dinwiddy
BERGSON Leszek Kolakowski
BERKELEY J. O. Urmson
THE BUDDHA Michael Carrithers
BURKE C. B. Macpherson
CERVANTES P. E. Russell
CLAUSEWITZ Michael Howard
COBBETT Raymond Williams
COLERIDGE Richard Holmes
DARWIN Jonathan Howard
DESCARTES Tom Sorell
DIDEROT Peter France
GEORGE ELIOT Rosemary Ashton
ENGELS Terrell Carver
ERASMUS James McConica
FREUD Anthony Storr
GALILEO Stillman Drake
GIBBON J. W. Burrow
GOETHE T. J. Reed
HEGEL Peter Singer
HOBBES Richard Tuck
HOMER Jasper Griffin
HUME A. J. Ayer

JESUS Humphrey Carpenter
KANT Roger Scruton
KIERKEGAARD Patrick Gardiner
LAMARCK L. J. Jordanova
LEIBNIZ G. MacDonald Ross
LOCKE John Dunn
MACHIAVELLI Quentin Skinner
MALTHUS Donald Winch
MARX Peter Singer
MENDEL Vitezslav Orel
MONTAIGNE Peter Burke
MONTESQUIEU Judith N. Shklar
THOMAS MORE Anthony Kenny
WILLIAM MORRIS Peter Stansky
MUHAMMAD Michael Cook
NEWMAN Owen Chadwick
PAINE Mark Philp
PAUL E. P. Sanders
PETRARCH Nicholas Mann
PLATO R. M. Hare
PROUST Derwent May
RUSKIN George P. Landow
SCHILLER T. J. Reed
SCHOPENHAUER Christopher Janaway
SHAKESPEARE Germaine Greer
ADAM SMITH D. D. Raphael
SPINOZA Roger Scruton
VICO Peter Burke
VIRGIL Jasper Griffin
WITTGENSTEIN A. C. Grayling
WYCLIF Anthony Kenny

Forthcoming

JOSEPH BUTLER R. G. Frey
COPERNICUS Owen Gingerich
DURKHEIM Frank Parkin
GODWIN Alan Ryan
JOHNSON Pat Rogers
JUNG Anthony Stevens
LINNAEUS W. T. Stearn

NEWTON P. M. Rattansi
ROUSSEAU Robert Wokler
RUSSELL A. C. Grayling
SOCRATES Bernard Williams
TOCQUEVILLE Larry Siedentop

and others

Henry Chadwick

Augustine

Oxford   New York

OXFORD UNIVERSITY PRESS

Oxford University Press, Walton Street, Oxford OX2 6DP

Oxford New York Toronto
Delhi Bombay Calcutta Madras Karachi
Kuala Lumpur Singapore Hong Kong Tokyo
Nairobi Dar es Salaam Cape Town
Melbourne Auckland Madrid

and associated companies in
Berlin Ibadan

Oxford is a trade mark of Oxford University Press

First published 1986 as an Oxford University Press paperback
and simultaneously in a hardback edition

British Library Cataloguing in Publication Data
Data available
ISBN 0-19-287534-5

Library of Congress Cataloging in Publication Data
Chadwick, Henry, 1920-
Augustine. (Past masters)
Bibliography: p. Includes index.
1. Augustine, Saint, Bishop of Hippo I. Title
II. Series
B655.Z7C46 1986 189.2 85-21560

ISBN 0-19-287534-5

7 9 10 8

Printed in Great Britain by
Biddles Ltd
Guildford and King's Lynn

Contents

NOTE: This book uses material from the Larkin Stuart Lectures, Toronto 1980, and the Sarum Lectures, Oxford 1982-3.

Abbreviations

Ac	*Contra Academicos*
B	*De baptismo*
BC	*De bono conjugali*
BV	*De beata vita*
C	*Confessiones*
CD	*De civitate Dei*
CE	*De consensu evangelistarum*
CG	*De correptione et gratia*
CR	*De catechizandis rudibus*
DDC	*De doctrina christiana*
DEP	*Contra duas epistulas Pelagianorum*
DP	*De dono perseverantiae*
E	*Epistulae*
EJo	*In epistulam Johannis*
EP	*Contra Epistulam Parmeniani*
F	*Contra Faustum Manichaeum*
GC	*De gratia Christi et de peccato originali*
GL	*De Genesi ad litteram*
J	*Contra Julianum Pelagianum*
Jo	*Tractatus in Evangelium Johannis*
LA	*De libero arbitrio*
M	*De moribus ecclesiae catholicae et de moribus Manichaeorum*
N	*De natura et gratia*
O	*De ordine*
P	*Enarrationes in Psalmos*
PM	*De peccatorum meritis*
QA	*De quantitate animae*
QH	*Quaestiones de Heptateucho*
QS	*De diversis quaestionibus ad Simplicianum*
R	*Retractationes*
S	*Sermones*
SL	*De spiritu et littera*
Sol	*Soliloquia*
T	*De Trinitate*
VR	*De vera religione*

1 The formation of Augustine's mind: Cicero, Mani, Plato, Christ

A short introduction to Augustine's thought cannot also offer biography. Partly because he wrote the most famous and influential of all ancient autobiographies, the psychology and personality of the man have naturally attracted concentrated attention. Among ancient men he had an unsurpassed power to articulate feelings. His writings are also a major source for the social history of his age. This book cannot be about that side of him, but concerns the making of his mind. That making was a drawn-out process; for he changed his mind on some points and developed his position on others. He described himself as 'a man who writes as he progresses and who progresses as he writes' (E 143). The shifts were closely related to the pressure of successive controversies in which he played a part, and reference to the historical setting is therefore essential for understanding. But beyond this we are not here concerned with his 'life and times'.

Aurelius Augustinus was born in AD 354 and died in 430. He lived all but five years of his life in Roman north Africa, and for the last thirty-four years was bishop of a busy seaport, Hippo, now Annaba in Algeria. At Hippo only bishop Augustine had books, and his own family background was not one of high culture. That culture he acquired through education. By his writings, the surviving bulk of which exceeds that of any other ancient author, he came to exercise pervasive influence not only on contemporaries but also on the West since his time. The extent of that influence can be summarized, in telegraphic style, by listing the debates which have been part of this man's legacy:

(1) The theology and philosophy of the medieval schoolmen and of the creators of medieval universities were rooted in Augustinian ideas of the relation between faith

and reason. When Peter Lombard compiled his *Sentences* (1155) to provide a basic textbook of theology, a very high proportion was drawn from Augustine. So too his contemporary Gratian cited many texts from him in making the West's principal handbook of canon law.

2 The aspirations of all western mystics have never escaped his influence, above all because of the centrality of the love of God in his thinking. He first saw the paradox that love, which is in quest of personal happiness, necessarily implies some self-renunciation and the pain of being made what one is not.

3 The Reformation found its mainspring in criticizing medieval Catholic piety as resting more on human effort than on divine grace. The Counter-Reformation replied that one can affirm the sovereignty of God's grace without also denying the freedom of the will and the moral value ('merit') of good conduct. Both sides in the controversy appealed on a huge scale to texts of Augustine.

4 The eighteenth century found itself passionately divided between those who asserted the perfectibility of man and those who saw human nature as held down by a dead weight of personal and collective egotism; in other words by what Augustine called 'original sin'. The men of the Enlightenment thought the actual perfecting of man hindered by belief in original sin and disliked Augustine very much. They were displeased when the philosopher Kant, who had so eloquently proclaimed the Enlightenment principle that one must dare to think for oneself, decisively assented to the belief that human nature is distorted by a pervasive radical evil.

5 In reaction against the Enlightenment the Romantic movement identified the heart of religion with feeling rather than with the conclusions of intellectual arguments. Augustine was not in the least anti-intellectual, but he did not think that intellect had the last word and he pioneered a highly positive evaluation of human feelings. We owe to him our use of the word 'heart' in this sense.

2

(6) He was the most acute of Christian Platonists and did much to lay the foundations for the synthesis between Christianity and classical theism stemming from Plato and Aristotle. Plotinus in the third century AD deeply influenced him by his systematization of the Platonic tradition, but Augustine also became one of the most penetrating of all critics of this philosophical tradition to which he himself owed so much.

(7) He saw more clearly than anyone before him (or for a long time after him) that issues of supreme importance are raised by the problem of the relation of words to the reality they attempt to describe. He was a pioneer in the critical study of non-verbal communication.

Anselm, Aquinas, Petrarch (never without a pocket copy of the *Confessions*), Luther, Bellarmine, Pascal, and Kierkegaard all stand in the shade of his broad oak. His writings were among the favourite books of Wittgenstein. He was the *bête noire* of Nietzsche. His psychological analysis anticipated parts of Freud: he first discovered the existence of the 'sub-conscious'.

He was 'the first modern man' in the sense that with him the reader feels himself addressed at a level of extraordinary psychological depth and confronted by a coherent system of thought, large parts of which still make potent claims to attention and respect. He affected the way in which the West has subsequently thought about the nature of man and what we mean by the word 'God'. Although as a follower of Plato he was little concerned with the natural physical environment, and wrote with fear of scientific investigations conducted without reverence and in indifference to ethical considerations, yet the modern scientist's assumption that mathematical order and rationality are the supreme features of the world had no more eloquent advocate in antiquity than he. He therefore contributed something substantial to the attitude towards the created order which would make the emergence of modern science possible. On the other hand, he cannot be fairly read if he is treated as other than what he was, a man of the ancient world, whose mind and culture were altogether shaped by the literature and philosophy of Greece and Rome and whose conversion to Christianity set him in some degree at odds with the classical past. In relation to that past he stood as both critic and transmitter to the medieval and modern worlds.

Just as the Greeks assumed with some reason that no one had written poetry to surpass Homer, or history in a way that rivalled Herodotus and Thucydides, or philosophy which was not a series of footnotes to Plato, Aristotle, the Stoics, and Epicurus, so also the Romans attributed the status of a classical model to their own past masters— Cicero for prose and oratory, Virgil and Horace for poetry. In Augustine's time there were educated people who knew entire orations of Cicero, and the whole of Virgil, by heart. Because the invention of printing has made books relatively inexpensive compared with manuscripts, such feats of memory appear needless and almost incredible to us today, but in the ancient and medieval worlds much school education consisted of learning by rote at an impressionable age. Cicero's prose and Virgil's poetry were so profoundly stamped on Augustine's mind that he could seldom write many pages without some reminiscence or verbal allusion. In youth he also read with deep admiration Sallust's sombre histories of the Roman Republic and the comedies of Terence. These too were part of the literary air he naturally breathed, and into his prose he would frequently work some turn of phrase taken from classical Latin literature. Many such allusions have been identified only comparatively recently, and it is certain that there are more yet to be located.

Augustine was not unique in his age in possessing this high literary culture. His cultural background was that of Roman Africa, rich colonial provinces which had long enjoyed peace and prosperity with highly educated people who adorned their villas with noble mosaic and sculpture such as one can see in the Bardo Museum at Tunis. Since the Muslim conquest of the region more than 200 years after Augustine's death, the north and south sides of the Mediterranean have belonged to separate cultural if not commercial worlds, and have spoken different languages except during the relatively brief period of French domination in modern times. In Augustine's age both north and south belonged to a single world, and wrote and spoke a good Latin which the Africans pronounced with a marked regional accent. North Africa supplied Italy with much of its grain. A summer voyage from Carthage or Hippo to Puteoli (Pozzuoli) or Ostia was a short sea journey made by several ships every week, and contact with Italy was frequent and easy. The wealth of Roman Africa often exceeded that found in Italy even among well-to-do families, and the African provinces had a strong sense of being independent and of wanting to make their own decisions.

Roman Africa had produced distinguished writers: in the first century, Manilius wrote a verse handbook on astrology; in the second century there was Fronto, tutor to the emperor Marcus Aurelius; Apuleius of Madaura, best-selling author not only of the 'Golden Ass' (*Metamorphoses*) with its characteristic mixture of magic, religion, and sex, but also of long influential handbooks on Platonic philosophy; Aulus Gellius, author of the 'Attic Nights'—a kind of reader's digest guide to effective dinner-party conversation. In Augustine's age there was Macrobius, whose commentary on Scipio's Dream (the last book of Cicero's *Republic*) became a major source of information about Neoplatonic philosophy for the medieval West; also the self-consciously pagan Martianus Capella, who, probably after Augustine's lifetime, composed 'The Marriage of Philology and Mercury' to teach his readers the elements of the seven liberal arts and to show how their study can lead one up to heaven.

5

During the second century a vigorous Christian mission in North Africa established a large number of congregations for whose use the Greek Bible was translated into Latin. The converts included brilliant figures such as Tertullian at the end of the second century, creator of the vocabulary of western theology and master of witty polemic against pagan critics or dangerous heretics; and Cyprian, elected bishop of Carthage soon after his baptism, martyred ten years later in 258, insistent on upholding the ritual purity of the Catholic Church and on the juridical authority of the apostolic ministry. In the age of Constantine the Great early in the fourth century two African Christians wrote defences of their faith against philosophical critics; Arnobius and Lactantius were partly indebted to Greek Christian writers before them.

The population of Roman Africa was very mixed. On the farms the peasants were Berber and Phoenician, speaking Punic. At the seaports like Carthage and Hippo many of the traders were Greek-speaking with close links to Sicily and South Italy, at that age (and long afterwards) a largely Greek-speaking region. But Latin was the language of the educated and the army and the administration. The culture of Augustine's home and school was wholly Latin, though his mother Monica bore a Berber name.

Late Roman Carthage was a successful trading city. Its population had a taste not only for animal and gladiatorial fights in the amphitheatre but also for less bloody occasions such as poetry competitions and good plays at the theatre. The city possessed well-qualified jurists, physicians, and teachers of literature—'grammarians' as they were called. Augustine was not born and raised in this urban world. He was a provincial country boy, born at an inland hill town called Thagaste in the province of Numidia Consularis, a cross-roads and market in what is now eastern Algeria at Souk-Ahras. There his father Patrick owned a few acres and one or two slavegirls, but was far from being rich. Patrick died when Augustine was a teenager with a lot of adolescent problems. Augustine also had a brother and a sister, but whether he was the eldest or the second or the third child is a matter on which there is no evidence. Education at the local school at Thagaste, as at all such small towns, was in the hands of a single teacher. Augustine found the man more effective with the cane than in inspiring his pupils with interest in their studies. Soon he passed on to another teacher at nearby Madaura. After Patrick's death he went on to Carthage, financed by a wealthy neighbour, Romanianus.

Augustine later looked back on his school days as a miserable experience, valuable only as a training for the conflicts, injustices, and disappointments of adult life. A highly sensitive and bookish boy, he felt he had largely educated himself by his reading in great authors. The punishments endured by children, however deserved, actually benefited only those disposed to be benefited, and left others merely resentful and even more anti-social than before. He never wrote with admiration or gratitude about any of his teachers.

As a schoolboy at Thagaste he began to learn Greek. Although he disliked the toil of learning the language, he was soon able to use a Greek book whenever necessary, and in his maturity he was competent to make his own translation of quite technical philosophical texts. But he never dreamed of acquiring a mastery of Homer and Greek literature, as a number of late Roman aristocrats did. He shared a feeling not uncommon in the Latin West of late antiquity that the West ought by now to have intellectual self-respect. It needed to stand on its own two feet and should do more than merely adapt Greek masterpieces for inferior Latin speakers. People did not then know or wish to notice that their hero Virgil owed a vast amount to Homer. They were, however, aware that in philosophy the Greeks were and remained the supreme masters. Cicero and Seneca had composed dialogues and 'letters' adapting Greek philosophical debates for the instruction of the Romans.

Cicero's philosophical dialogues were a mine of clearly set out information about the debates between the different schools, and in his twenties Augustine came to know their content very well.

Though not ignorant of Greek, Augustine was always more comfortable with a Latin version if that happened to be available. He was familiar with the *Categories* of Aristotle, which were available to him in Latin, and with his investigations of the laws of valid inference. The knotty problem of 'future contingents' discussed in the notorious ninth chapter of Aristotle's tract on *Interpretation* was familiar to him also. In agreement with the Neoplatonists of his time he used language about the uncertainties of the future which was more determinist than the followers of Aristotle liked; he wanted to say that events which to us are 'contingent' (i.e. they would not have occurred unless something happened to cause them) are not uncertain to God (F 26. 4–5). In other words, though we have minds too limited to see it, the future is as unalterable as the past. Augustine was particularly interested in Stoic logic and ethical assertions. He was fascinated by the question of how far language communicates meaning about reality. He was capable of acute analysis of the problems contained in Epicurus' hedonist contention that by 'right' and 'wrong' we really mean 'pleasing' and 'displeasing'.

Paradoxically, the Greek thinker whose work most deeply entered his bloodstream was Plato, of whose works singularly little was available in Latin. Cicero had translated about half the *Timaeus*, and on this dialogue Calcidius in the fourth century had composed an elaborate commentary which Augustine could have known (but probably did not). It would not have been difficult for him to find Greek copies of Platonic dialogues at either Carthage or Rome, where he taught for a time. Both cities had citizens who knew the language. But he never seems to have made any direct study of the original text.

The form of Platonic philosophy which eventually (when

he was 31) captured his mind was the 'modern' Platonism which we now call Neoplatonism, taught a century earlier by Plotinus (205–270) to an esoteric circle, and then vigorously presented to the public by his acute pupil, editor, and biographer Porphyry of Tyre (*c.*250–*c.*305). Though Plotinus did his teaching at Rome and Porphyry lived part of his life in Sicily, both men wrote exclusively in Greek. Despite the abstraction and complexity of the ideas, Plotinus and Porphyry came to have enormous influence, in the Latin West quite as much as in the Greek East. In Plotinus, during the flush of his first enthusiasm for Platonism, Augustine declared he saw 'Plato come to life again' (Ac. 3.41), a phrase which accurately reflects what Plotinus himself set out to do, for he regarded Plato as more than a man with great independent powers of thought. Plato ranked for him as an authority.

Absorbing the principal doctrines of Stoic ethics and, in Porphyry's hands, much Aristotelian logic as well, Neoplatonism became altogether dominant over all other philosophical positions in late antiquity. Works by both Plotinus and Porphyry were translated into Latin by Marius Victorinus, an African who taught rhetoric and philosophy in Rome and at the height of his reputation, about the time that Augustine was born, had startled a largely pagan aristocracy by being baptized. Victorinus also translated some logical works by Aristotle and Porphyry, notably the *Introduction* to Aristotle's logic composed by Porphyry with such clarity and terse precision that the book became a standard handbook for a millennium.

Cicero

The most potent initial influence guiding the young Augustine in philosophical matters came from Cicero's dialogues. Of the many works of Cicero which Augustine knew intimately, one dialogue called *Hortensius*, vindicating the necessity of philosophical thinking for any critical judgement even for someone engaged in public and

9

political life, exercised an extraordinary, catalytic effect. In the works of his old age he was still to be quoting phrases from this book which he first read as a nineteen-year-old student at Carthage. Cicero partly adapted for the Roman world an exhortation to study philosophy written by no less than Aristotle himself. Cicero's ideal was personal self-sufficiency and an awareness that happiness, which everyone seeks, is not found in a self-indulgent life of pleasure, which merely destroys both self-respect and true friendships. Contemplating the paradox that everyone sets out to be happy and the majority are thoroughly wretched, Cicero concluded with the pregnant suggestion that man's misery may be a kind of judgement of providence, and our life now may even be an atonement for sins in a prior incarnation. The *Hortensius* also included a warning that the pursuit of bodily pleasure in food, drink, and sex, is distracting for the mind in pursuit of higher things.

Augustine was never a glutton or a drinker; but his sexual drive was strong. At the age of seventeen to eighteen at Carthage he had already taken to his bed a girl-friend of servile or low social class, a steady relationship which put an end to adolescent adventures. For over thirteen years Augustine lived with her entirely faithfully. She soon produced an initially unwanted but in the event much loved son, whom they called Adeodatus or 'God's gift', equivalent to Theodore or Jonathan or its Punic cognate form. The boy turned out very clever, but died at the age of seventeen.

The immediate effect of reading *Hortensius* was to make Augustine think seriously about ethical and religious issues. His father had been a pagan, baptized only on his deathbed. He was hot-tempered and not always faithful to his wife; Augustine betrays no sign of having felt close to him. His mother, on the other hand, was devout in Christian faith and practice, daily at prayers in her local church, often guided by dreams and visions. She had made him a catechumen in infancy. As a sceptical teenager he used occasionally to attend church services with her, but found himself mainly engaged in catching the eye of the girls on the other side of the basilica. At Carthage aged nineteen he found that the seriousness of the questions raised by Cicero, especially about the quest for happiness, moved him to pick up a Latin Bible. He was repelled by the obscurity of its content and the barbarous style of the rather primitive version made by half-educated missionaries in the second century. The Old Latin Bible (the reconstruction of which by modern scholars has been a remarkable critical operation) was not a book to impress a man whose mind was full of elegant Ciceronian diction and Virgilian turns of phrase, and who enjoyed good plays at the theatre. In disgust Augustine turned away from what seemed a naïve myth about Adam and Eve and from the doubtful morality of the Israelite patriarchs. To any prospect of his returning to the Church of his mother, the incompatibility between the two genealogies of Jesus in Matthew and Luke gave the final *coup de grâce* (S 51.6).

So Augustine looked elsewhere for help. He was drawn to astrology, which seemed to offer a guide to live by without looking too like a religion, and then to the occult theosophy taught more than a century earlier by Mani (AD 216–77).

Mani

The religion of Mani, or Manicheism, expressed in poetic form a revulsion from the material world, and became the rationale for an ultra-ascetic morality. The Manichees regarded 'the lower half of the body' as the disgusting work of the devil, the very prince of darkness. Sex and the dark were intimately associated in Mani's mind, and the Dark was the very essence of evil. One would not expect such a religion to have attractions for a young man to whom sex was important (unless it were that one could attribute all one's lower impulses to the powers of darkness and disown personal responsibility). However, the Manichee community consisted of two classes or grades of adherent. Absolute celibacy was required only of the higher grade, the

11

Elect. Mere Hearers, of whom Augustine became one, were allowed sexual relations at 'safe' periods of the month, and were expected to take steps to avoid conceiving a child; but if a child arrived, that was not a ground for expulsion from the society. Hearers therefore were allowed to live with wives or, as in Augustine's case, concubines, but were not encouraged to think of sexuality in any positive light. It was the devil's invention.

Mani denied any authority to the Old Testament with its presupposition of the goodness of the material order of things and of its Maker. He deleted as interpolations all texts in the New Testament which assumed either the order and goodness of matter or the inspiration and authority of the Old Testament scriptures. Otherwise he thought his expurgated New Testament a sound book. He generously acknowledged truth in all religious systems, and rejected orthodox catholic Christianity for being too exclusive and negative towards other religious myths and forms of worship. Yet he wanted to be considered Christian, while asserting that his revelation founded 'a distinct religion'. He was a 'heretic' in the strict sense of a person wanting to stay within the community while reinterpreting its fundamental documents and beliefs in ways unacceptable to the main body, and persisting therein when asked to correct himself. He employed some biblical themes and terms, and allowed a redemptive role to Jesus—only he understood Jesus as a symbol of the plight of all humanity rather than as a historical person who walked the earth and was crucified. A quasi-divine redeemer could not in truth have been physically born or killed (an opinion anticipating Islamic doctrine); the crucifixion was no kind of actuality but a mere symbol for the suffering which is the universal human condition.

Mani interpreted everything he took from Christianity within a dualistic and pantheistic framework: this is seen in the immensely complex and elaborate mythology in which he cast his doctrine. The central question for him was the origin of evil. He explained evil as resulting from a primeval and still continuing cosmic conflict between Light and Dark, these terms being both symbol and physical reality. The forces of good and evil in the world have strengths and weaknesses such that neither side can vanquish the other. In consequence of the damage inflicted by the powers of Dark on the realm of Light, little fragments of God, or Soul, have become scattered throughout the world in all living things, including animals and plants. Melons and cucumbers were deemed to contain a particularly large ingredient of divinity, and were therefore prominent in the diet of Manichee Elect. Food laws for the Elect were elaborate, and wine strictly forbidden. Manichee teachers and missionaries liked to recruit from members of the Church. The infiltration of Manichee notions could be detected when Christians at the eucharist accepted the host but not the chalice. Church people could be specially impressed by the fine parchment and calligraphy of Manichee sacred books and by the special solemnity of their music.

Although Mani accorded a high place in his myth to Jesus, supreme and infallible teaching office was located for his community not in Jesus nor in old Jewish books but in Mani himself, the Apostle of God, the very Paraclete foretold by Jesus as coming along later to reveal truths for which the altogether too Jewish disciples were unprepared. Mani had no place whatever for the particularity which the Church inherited from its Jewish matrix. By a bizarre twist he presented his lush, partly erotic mythology with the claim that it was a rational, coherent account of revealed truth, in strong contrast to the simple faith of orthodox Christians who believed on mere authority. Manichee propaganda devoted much attention to onslaughts upon the morality and historical accuracy of the Old Testament and those parts of the New Testament which seemed too Jewish for Manichee taste. Above all, the Manichees urged that they had the only satisfactory answer to the problem of evil:

13

it was an ineradicable force inherent in the physicality of the material world. No one could plausibly hold that the ultimate author of so uncomfortable a world could be both omnipotent and truly good. If the argument was to be coherent, either the omnipotence or the goodness must be sacrificed. Manichee teachers took it for granted that everyone knew without further definition or inquiry just what is meant by 'evil'.

During a full ten years, in teaching posts first at Carthage and then at Rome, Augustine remained associated with the Manichees. A combative critic of Catholic orthodoxy and conscious of his own intellectual superiority to members of the Church, whose bishops he held in contempt for their lack of education and critical inquiry, he converted many friends to share his Manichee beliefs. But during his twenties he was not only teaching Latin literature and the arts of rhetoric. He was also reflecting on philosophical issues and logical problems to which studies in rhetoric naturally led. Mounting doubts came to beset him. Was Mani right when he asserted that the supremely good Light-power was weak and impotent in conflict with Dark? How could one properly worship a deity so powerless and humiliated? Moreover, the Manichees myth gave a large role to the two great and good lights of sun and moon and held a dogmatic position about the explanation of eclipses, namely that sun and moon are then using special veils to shut out the distressing sight of cosmic battles. Augustine was disturbed to find that the Manichee account was at variance with that of the best astronomers. One might demythologize orthodox Christianity and still have something of great importance left; Augustine felt that this was not true of Manicheism, where the myth was of the essence. Growing disillusion with the sect reached a climax when he put his doubts before a teacher held in high regard by the Manichees, Faustus. He found the man's eloquence greater than his capacity for thought. Further, the moral life of the

Elect, who claimed sinless perfection, turned out to be less celibate than he had supposed.

He began to look about for alternatives to Manicheism. Already he had developed an interest in combining Manichee beliefs about the balance of good and evil with Neopythagorean ideas about proportion as an element in the beauty of the whole, about the good 'monad' (one is one and all alone and evermore shall be so) in contrast to the evil of infinite plurality. In his mid twenties he even wrote a book on this subject which in later retrospect he scorned as a half-baked piece of ill-digested stuff (C iv.20–7). Increasingly his doubts plunged him into suspense of judgement. He became intensely interested in the theory of knowledge: how do we know anything? How can we be absolutely sure? How do we communicate with each other when words can be misleading, or construed in a sense quite different from that intended by the speaker? Is everyday language, so frequently defying the rules of logic, a source of light or fog?

In this hesitant state of mind Augustine devoured books by sceptical philosophers, dogmatically assertive about the uncertainty and inconclusiveness of all received opinions, of sense-perception, and of the power of words to tell one anything important that one does not really know already. This was his mind when he arrived at Milan in 384 as the city's new professor of rhetoric but with hopes of rising higher still. Milan was the imperial residence. If, despite Italian smiles at his African vowels, he could speak so eloquently as to attract favourable attention at court, and if he could gain the support of influential officials, perhaps he might aspire to be nominated as governor of a province (C vi.19). Admittedly there were obstacles to the ambition. He was a middle-class provincial without the recommendation of personal wealth to back him. Moreover, he still had living with him his 'common-law wife', his Carthaginian girlfriend, Adeodatus' mother. What would raise no eyebrow when done by a city professor of rhetoric might not be acceptable at government house. His widowed mother Monica, who had devotedly pursued him to Milan, saw that her son's much loved but uneducated partner in bed and board was a fatal hindrance to his secular desire for distinction and honour. Eventually the woman was sent back to Carthage. The parting was with great pain on both sides. Augustine was then engaged to marry a youthful heiress, whose dowry would facilitate the realization of his hopes. Until she was old enough to marry, Augustine turned for consolation to a temporary mate; she had no deep significance for him. His feelings were numb.

At Milan Augustine met, for the first time in his life, a Christian intellectual with ability not far short of his own: Ambrose the bishop, a man of high education, who also knew his way about the corridors of power at the court. He received Augustine kindly, and Monica held him in deep respect as a pastor. Before becoming bishop in 374, he had been provincial governor of that part of northern Italy. His education in an aristocratic and Christian household had made him fluent in Greek. For his sermons he drew ideas and inspiration not only from Greek Christian theologians like Basil of Caesarea and the Jewish theologian Philo, elder contemporary of St Paul, but also from Plotinus. Ambrose's debt to Plotinus was combined with caution about pagan philosophy as a guide to truth.

Another Christian intellectual at Milan who influenced Augustine was an older man named Simplicianus, through whom he became drawn into a group of laymen of high education and social standing, who met to read Plotinus and Porphyry. They much admired Marius Victorinus, whose last years had been devoted to the deployment of Neoplatonic logic in defence of orthodox Trinitarian belief. Augustine was never greatly influenced by the obscure theological writings of Victorinus. But his readings in Plotinus and Porphyry, translated by Victorinus, set his mind on fire. That may seem surprising to the modern reader, for whom Neoplatonism can easily seem intricate and esoteric. The Neoplatonic philosophy of Being has presuppositions or axioms very different from those of modern scientific method: its starting point is mind, not matter.

Plotinus and Porphyry

Porphyry's biography of Plotinus portrays the awe in which the great philosopher was held, at least in his inner circle of pupils. Porphyry wrote the biography to accompany his edition of Plotinus, partly because he wanted everyone to know how right his hero had been to entrust him with the publication of his treatises; how profoundly Plotinus had admired his pupil's critical mind and capacity for composing inspired ecstatic verses; and how at the age of 68 Porphyry himself had on one blissful occasion attained mystical union with the One, an experience which came only four times in life even to the divinely illuminated Plotinus. Plotinus is represented as a man of unique genius, whose guardian spirit was no inferior power, and whose mind never relaxed its concentration on the highest peaks of the intellect.

Like his elder Christian contemporary Origen, Plotinus lived an ascetic life of minimal food and sleep, given to vegetarianism and no baths. 'He always seemed ashamed of being in the body', and never celebrated his birthday. To his numerous male and female pupils Plotinus became a father figure, consulted on major and minor decisions of life. He had a preternatural discernment of mendacity and, like Christian bishops, was asked to arbitrate in disputes. He successfully dissuaded the highly-strung Porphyry from suicide.

In his philosophical system Plotinus set out to paint a kind of word-picture of the entire structure of things on the assumption that there is intimate correspondence between reality and the process of human thought. He attached high importance to the dialectic of Plato's dialogues, *Parmenides* and *Sophist*, especially Plato's analysis of identity and difference. That is, if we say x and y are 'the same', we imply distinction between them if the assertion of identity is to be interesting. Conversely, to point out that x and y are different implies an underlying bond of identity between them. So, beyond the multiplicity and the differences perceived and experienced in this world, there lies a unity and a permanence. Likewise the world of perceived appearances is one of perpetual change; but change presupposes a substratum which remains permanent.

Plato attributed changelessness to the higher world of Being grasped by the mind, in contrast to the ever-changing flux of Becoming discerned by the bodily senses. Hence Plato's theory of Forms (or Ideas), eternal absolutes: whatever in this world we call just or good or beautiful or true, is so in so far as it derives from the respective absolute. The Forms are the objective, constant, and universally valid reality. Moreover, these universals are perceived not by the five bodily senses, but by an austerely mathematical process of pure mental abstraction. Bloodless as these abstractions may appear, Platonism understands these universals as highly causative: individual existents cannot be accounted for in isolation, but only as members of a prior class. Therefore, for a Platonist, the universal is more real than any particular instance—a doctrine countered by Aristotle with the criticism that universals are mental classifications with reality only as they are embodied in particular existents. In his 'Introduction' Porphyry pursued his theme of reconciling Plato and Aristotle by juxtaposing these two opinions and carefully abstaining from giving a verdict between them.

Aristotle had been interested in self-consciousness, in which the knower and the object known are identical. Plotinus took this observation a stage further to form a theology, many themes of which came to seem self-evident axioms to Augustine. At the summit of the hierarchy of being is the One, God, the unknowable and Absolute, yet apprehended by the soul as a presence transcending all knowing. In the great chain or continuum of being which Plotinus identified as the structure of things, the higher level is cause of whatever is immediately lower. Plotinus spoke of the evolution or development of the hierarchy of being as 'emanation', a strongly physical image. In the process of emanation there is gradual loss; for every effect is slightly inferior to its cause. Nevertheless the imperfection inherent in its inferiority can be overcome as it returns towards its cause. And the cause itself is always undiminished by its timeless giving of existence to the inferior effect.

This way of thinking of causative emanation in the great chain of being enabled Plotinus to achieve several things at once. On the one hand it solved the problem of how to keep the transcendent One and the world from losing all relation to each other, without the Absolute ceasing to be Absolute, and without the world logically dropping out of existence altogether. It expressed a kind of redemption by 'conversion' to the source of being. On the other hand, it alleviated a problem which caused acute mental gymnastics for all Platonists, namely answering the question how evil could ever have entered into the continuum of things, when that was an overflow of supreme goodness and power.

Plotinus taught that at the apex of the hierarchy are three divine existences: the One, Mind, and Soul. The One is supremely Good, and therefore all lower levels of the hierarchy below the One must be also distinct from the Good; in short, less than perfectly good. Even Mind has some inferiority about it, some delusions about its own grandeur. Soul, still further down the scale, has the power to produce matter. Matter, being at the opposite extremity of the hierarchy from the good One, is in cosmic terms utter evil, formless non-being.

The Neoplatonists cordially hated theosophy, and its Manichee form more than all. Plotinus' treatise 'Against the Gnostics' (ii.9) inaugurated a series of Neoplatonic essays in polemic against Manicheism. By seeing the cosmos as a great chain of being, Plotinus could declare that evil is no more than a defect of being-and-goodness, inherent in the mere fact of an inferior level. But two other explanations of evil were also prominent in his thinking. Of these the first answer looked towards the consequence of misused free choice grounded in a potentiality for weakness in the soul. The second answer looked towards matter. Weakness in the soul tended to make it absorbed in external and material things. Thereby the cosmic, non-moral evil of defect of being inherent in matter becomes a root of moral evil in the soul. 'Without matter there can be no moral evil' (Plotinus i.8,14). The presence of matter to the soul brings out its weakness and causes its fall. At the same time, Plotinus wished to speak of the coming forth and descent of the soul as necessary for the fulfilment of its potential powers and for the service that soul has to render to the inferior world of the senses (iv.8,4–5). It is fair to deduce that even Plotinus failed to achieve a clear and consistent position. After his conversion Augustine sought to correct Plotinus' mistakes.

The doctrines of Porphyry were similar to those of his master Plotinus. In the Neoplatonic school there was disagreement about the cult of the gods. Plotinus and Porphyry felt reserve towards participation in sacrifices to propitiate the spirits. Porphyry wrote a treatise *On the Soul's Return* (that is, to God), to Augustine profoundly exciting reading; this presented a compromise position. He allowed that good philosophy could be extracted at shrines from inspired oracles uttered by Apollo through his prophetesses. But he wrote critically of fellow-pagans who supposed that the soul could be purified directly through participation in temple sacrifices or external ritual acts. Animal sacrifices were too earth-bound. Moreover, the custom of eating the meat afterwards was not congenial to vegetarian principles. So Porphyry urged that the soul's purging could be achieved

only by 'flight from the body', to which it had become
united by a chapter of sad accidents. By abstinence from
meat and from sexual activity, the soul could be gradually
emancipated from its bodily fetters.   3

Porphyry taught that happiness consists in wisdom,
which is found by obeying the ancient command of Delphi,
'Know yourself'. Admittedly, wickedness in the soul makes
man impotent to practise continual intellectual contemplation, so that at best such moments are transitory. But 'exercise yourself to return to yourself; gather from the body all
the spiritual elements dispersed and reduced to a mass of
bits and pieces'. 'The soul is thrust into poverty, the more
that its ties to the flesh are strengthened. But it can become
truly rich by discovering its true self, which is intellect.'
'Our end is to attain the contemplation of Being.' 'He who
knows God has God present to him. He who does not know
is absent from God who is everywhere present.'
Augustine's *Confessions* echo this language.

Porphyry taught that God contains all things but is contained by nothing. The One is present to all that par-
ticipates in the existence flowing from its source in God.
Goodness must be self-diffusive. But all plurality depends
upon and seeks to return to higher and prior unity. In the
hierarchy of being it is axiomatic that it is good to exist, and
that degrees of being are also degrees of goodness. Porphyry
wrote that 'everything which has being is good in so far as
it has being; even the body has its own beauty and unity'.
(Augustine says the same, VR 40.) Between material things
and the higher realms of intelligible reality, the soul oc-
cupies a median position. By neglect and an inexplicable act
of self-assertive defiance it is capable of sinking to pride, envy, and carnal things. But by ascetic restraint and by in-
trospective contemplation, the soul can ascend to its true   3
fulfilment. This fulfilment is 'the enjoyment of God'. This
last phrase Augustine was to make his own.

Porphyry drew from Plotinus the concept that at the apex
of the chain of being there lies, beyond the reach of our five

senses, a divine Triad of being, life, and intelligence, all reciprocal, defined as a unity within which one can discern distinctions. The structure of things is that of a rhythmic procession out from the ultimate principle of being, from potentiality to actuality, from abstract to concrete, from identity to that otherness which is also a diminution in the level of being. The destiny of eternal souls is to return whence they have come. Souls are inherently immortal. The doctrine of return or conversion is the meaning of Plato's doctrine of Reminiscence, i.e. that all knowledge is a recalling to mind of what one once knew (in a previous existence) but had forgotten. This doctrine the Neoplatonists, and Augustine after them, largely replaced by the notion of divine illumination directly shining within the soul.

Near the end of his life Porphyry (who is reported by some Christian writers to have been a Christian in his youth and then to have apostatized) composed a lengthy and bitter attack on Christian beliefs and on the historical trust-worthiness of the biblical books. His book against the Christians was not known to Augustine. Porphyry's works, however, may fairly be described as offering an alternative religious philosophy, designed, whether consciously or unconsciously, to provide a rival and antidote to Christianity.

The Milan group of Platonists gripped their new professor of rhetoric with Victorinus' translations of tracts by Plotinus and Porphyry. The language Augustine found there about the problem of evil and about mystical experience of the immaterial transcendent realm had an immense impact. The Neoplatonists were telling him that the soul has an immediate and inherent power of self-knowledge; moreover, that this power can be realized only as and when the perceptions of the five senses are set aside and the mind undergoes a purification, by dialectic, which purges it of physical images and elevates it to the beatific vision of which Plato spoke. They believed this to be a natural power of the soul, realized as it gradually opens itself to divine light and truth.

Augustine was later to describe, in the seventh book of the *Confessions*, how at Milan he attempted deep meditation on the Neoplatonic method. Platonism liberated him from the Manichee notion of God as subtle luminous matter. By introspection in solitude and by practising the way of dialectical regress from external to internal, from inferior and physical to superior and mental, he briefly attained a vision of eternal truth and unchanging beauty. He was disappointed by the extreme transience of an experience so profound, and by the fact that afterwards he found himself as consumed with pride and lust as before. Nevertheless, he knew that in that 'flash of a trembling glance' he had attained a dazzling glimpse of the immutable and eternal Being, an immaterial reality wholly transcending his own all too changeable mind (C vii.23). There is no hint of a suggestion in his later retrospect written as a Christian that this preconversion experience was anything less than authentic. Later in the *Confessions* (xi.11) he would use almost identical language about the union of love and dread, the dread induced by the contemplation of the unapproachable Other so distant and 'unlike', the love by the awareness of the Other who is so similar and so near; the dread corresponding to negative and impersonal attributes, the love asking to be expressed in frankly personal terms.

At the heart of the experience he described lay the conviction that the finite creature has an insatiable longing for a fulfilment that can be found only in what lies beyond itself, and indeed beyond human capacity for definition or description.

Neoplatonic exhortations to suppress the passions and the physical senses took Augustine back to Cicero's warning that sexual indulgence does not make for mental clarity. Porphyry's tract on vegetarianism taught that, 'just as priests at temples must abstain from sexual intercourse in order to be ritually pure at the time of offering sacrifice, so also the individual soul needs to be equally pure to attain to the vision of God.' Augustine knew himself to be 'dragged down by the weight of a carnal life'. He was not a Christian; yet it was through Christians like Simplicianus of Milan that he had discovered an experience of deep psychological importance to him, giving him both a sense of total certitude and also an awareness of his own impermanence in contrast to the eternal Being of the One. He found himself torn in a struggle between a meditative philosophy which called his soul to higher things than the body, and his habit of sexual activity, by which he felt himself bound and in which he had long found a source of physical, if not psychological, satisfaction. He began to hope and pray that he would eventually attain continence, 'but not yet' (C viii.16). It was both a comfort and a stimulus that Cicero's *Hortensius* had taught that 'the mere search for higher happiness, not merely its actual attainment, is a prize beyond all human wealth or honour or physical pleasure'.

Towards conversion

If the paradoxical effect of Cicero's *Hortensius* when he was nineteen had been to drive him to Manicheism, the effect of his Platonic readings when he was thirty-one was to impel him towards Porphyry's greatest object of hatred, the Church. The Neoplatonic circle at Milan was specially interested in parts of the New Testament, such as the prologue to St John's Gospel or St Paul's strongly Platonizing language in 2 Corinthians 3–4, which offered a biblical foundation for a Christian Platonism. The Christians in this group were concerned to interpret St Paul's epistle to the Romans in a way that averted Manichee determinism and dualism. As a Manichee Augustine had interpreted the apostle as being inconsistent not only with the Old Testament but also with himself. Pauline language about the conflict of flesh and spirit (Galatians 5 and Romans 7) was taken by the Manichees as a charter for their belief that the body's sexual impulses are at the root of all evil. The Milan Neoplatonists took a slightly less pessimistic view. Soon Augustine was convinced that from Plato to Christ was hardly more than a short and simple step, and that the teaching of the Church was in effect 'Platonism for the multitude', a pictorial and figurative way of addressing unphilosophical minds with the effect of making them rational at least in conduct. To the end of his days, long after his reservations about certain elements in the Platonic tradition had become specific and explicit, Augustine would not fail to make handsome acknowledgement of his indebtedness to the Neoplatonic books. As he lay dying at Hippo during the long Vandal siege of his city, his last recorded words were a quotation from Plotinus.

Neoplatonic spirituality and the stress on interiority and on liberation from the distractions of the external world, sharpened Augustine's feeling of being pulled in two different directions with his sexual drive as a downward pull. As he read the letters of St Paul, he began to think his condition wholly understood by the apostle. He found himself in a whirlpool of inward conflict. The consciousness of his wretchedness was one day poignantly enhanced as he walked in a Milan street past a laughing beggar happy under the anaesthetic of liquor (C vi.9). He realized that his feeling on contemplating the man was not pity but envy. The professor of rhetoric found that his copy of the Pauline letters was becoming important to him.

At the end of July 386 in the garden of the house in Milan where he was living with his mother and with his former pupil Alypius (a competent lawyer who in 386 was still shedding Manichee beliefs, and later became bishop of Thagaste), Augustine finally came to the point of decision. His health had become poor with asthmatic trouble on his chest and loss of voice; whether this was a symptom of his malaise or a contributory cause of his decision cannot be determined. He decided to abandon his teaching post, and therewith ambitions for a secular career. The crux was the abandonment of all intention to marry. Could he bring himself to live without a woman? From an African friend working in the court bureaucracy he learnt of the existence of a community of ascetics living in Milan and of the renunciation of wealth by Antony, the Egyptian hermit, whose Life had been written by Athanasius, bishop of Alexandria, and was quickly translated into Latin for western readers. If they could achieve continence, then he could also. Or was his will too weak?

According to the narrative in the eighth book of the *Confessions* written fourteen years later he picked up his copy of St Paul, opened it at random and, in the manner of those who sought guidance for the future from Virgil, took guidance from the first text he saw—the concluding words of Romans 13, contrasting sexual wantonness with the calling to 'put on Christ'. He described his decision in exquisite literary language, with echoes from the poet Persius, a striking phrase from Plotinus, and a symbolic allusion to fallen Adam in the garden of Eden. He recounted how he heard as it were a voice like a child's bidding him to 'pick up and read' (*tolle, lege*). How much of the narrative is plain prose and how much is literary or rhetorical decoration has been a matter of controversy. That there is a literary element is certain. It is also certain that in Milan at the end of July 386 he made a decision to abandon marriage and secular ambition and to be baptized. He resigned his city teaching post.

The conversion was no sudden flash, but the culminating point of many months of painful gestation. He himself was later to compare the process of conversion to pregnancy. The choice marked a shift more ethical than intellectual in content. The story told in the *Confessions* presupposes that in 386 he understood sexual passion as the one obstacle between his soul and union with eternal incorporeal truth. What Plotinus and Porphyry had taught him was now being made possible and actual with the help of a text from St Paul. Fifteen years later he would be writing of the 'illusion' some have that in this life it is possible for the human mind so to detach itself from the physical world as to grasp 'the unclouded light of unchanging truth' (CE iv.20).

Nevertheless, at the time he had the sensations of 'coming into harbour after a stormy passage'. Monica's prayers for his conversion and baptism were answered. The son of so many tears could not be lost.

A few months later he declared that, although old desires did not cease to disturb his dreams, nevertheless he was beginning to make progress, for he now regarded sexual union with revulsion as a 'bitter sweetness' (Sol. i.25). His ascetic aspirations did not make him wish to be a hermit. His longing was to be with a community of lay friends sharing his enthusiasm for Plato and St Paul with some Cicero (especially the *Tusculan Disputations*) thrown in. Eight months passed between his decision in the Milan garden and Easter 387 when he was baptized by Ambrose together with his natural son Adeodatus and his friend Alypius the lawyer. During these months he and Monica with a group of friends and pupils were lent a villa at Cassiciacum in the hills near Como. There he could recover his health and think out his position.

His conversion does not appear in his writings at the time as motivated by a desire to escape the painful uncertainties of philosophical scepticism by taking refuge in the dogmatic authority of the Church. The source of his misery and dissatisfaction lay in himself. Nevertheless the problem of authority was prominent in the controversies between Catholics and Manichees, and he acknowledged that he was submitting to Christ and his community. A claim to self-determination he came to see as pride (C x.58). From the autumn of 386 onwards his writings would contain frequent allusions to the Bible and Christian doctrine. At Cassiciacum he wrote of authority and reason as parallel routes to the truth, authority being Christ, reason being represented by Plato. Authority can give directions which reason subsequently understands. Authority is prior in time, reason prior in the order of reality. The well educated prefer to follow the philosophic path of reason; but even there reason cannot be sufficient to provide all the guidance needed. On the other hand, an exclusive reliance on authority must be beset by great danger. Without reason how can one discriminate between competing claims to authority? How can one distinguish between authentically divine authority and that of inferior spirits venerated by pagans who claim to predict the future by divination and soothsaying? The divine authority of Christ, however, is demonstrated by being simultaneously the highest reason. He is the very Wisdom of God, identical with the Mind of Plotinus' supreme Triad (O ii.26–7).

Finally, one must ask what specific ideas about God and man were accepted by Augustine in consequence of his baptism and confession of faith. Reduced to its most basic and skeletal elements, the Christian faith invited him to make the following affirmations. First, the ordered world stems from the supreme Good who is also the supreme Power, not merely the best that happens to exist, but a perfection such that our minds cannot even frame the idea of any superior being. Therefore 'he' is the proper object of awe and worship. We should not think of God as involved in a process of struggling from lower to higher as human beings do (and as the Manichee Light power), but rather as having a consistent creative and redemptive purpose in relation to the universe in general and the rational creation in particular. The supreme level in the ladder of value is the love which is the very nature of God.

Secondly, human nature as now experienced fails to correspond to the Creator's intentions. Human misery is perpetuated by social and individual egotisms, so that man is haunted by ignorance, mortality and the brevity of life, weakness of will, above all by the arrogant and wilful rejection of his true good. In short, humanity needs the remedy of eternal life and the forgiveness of sins, or restoration under the love of God.

Thirdly, the supreme God has acted within the time and history in which we live, and which 'he' transcends, bringing to us knowledge, life, strength, and (greatest gift of all) humility without which no one learns anything. This act has its culminating focus in Jesus, model to humanity by his life and wise teaching and by his unique filial relation to the supreme 'Father'. Jesus embodied the gift of God's love by the humility of his incarnation and death. Access to this movement of God to rescue fallen man is found through the assent of faith and through adhesion to the community of Jesus' followers, a structured community entrusted by him with the gospel and with sacramental covenant signs of water, bread, and wine. Thereby the Spirit of holiness unites man to God, to give hope for the life to come, of which Jesus' resurrection is the ultimate pledge, and to transform the individual's personal and moral life to be fit for the society of saints in the presence of God.

In these themes Christian preaching spoke to Augustine in strongly other-worldly terms which linked arms with Platonic morality and metaphysics. It was momentous that he brought together Plotinus' negative, impersonal language about the One or Absolute and the biblical concept of God as love, power, justice, and forgiveness. It is cardinal to theism that the mystery of God is known not only in the grandeur and glory of nature but also by a self-disclosure—on the analogy of a person making known to others what they could not find out for themselves. From 387 onwards Augustine took these ideas as first principles.

2　Liberal arts

Perhaps because Platonism contributed substantially to his conversion to Christianity, Augustine was at no time to draw sharp frontiers between philosophy and theology. He did not think of philosophic reason either as a mere hand-maid to religion or as a dangerous whore out to seduce the mind into supposing that it could attain its supreme end without God's help and grace. The prime subject of philosophy he defined as 'the study of God and the human soul' (Sol. i.7)—one notices the exclusion of the physical world. The motive which led people to philosophize he described in Ciceronian terms as simply the quest for happiness.

Neoplatonic ontology, or doctrine of being and of how things are, described in the last chapter, is pervasive throughout his writings. Only there are respects in which he modified the detail of it, which leaves the impression that in so far as he accepted the Platonic arguments, he always turned them to conclusions defined by his faith. It would perhaps be truer to say that he saw little reason to dissent from the Platonic tradition unless it was incompatible with the implications of the catholic creed. Naturally, he regarded the pagan Platonists as mistaken in accepting polytheism, everlasting world-cycles and the transmigration of souls. The ancient belief in reincarnation was altogether too fatalistic to be compatible with the concept of God as uniquely creative power, acting in redemption to bring his rational creation to its true end of fellowship with himself.

There were other points of disagreement which were less obvious but not less important. Despite the prominence of the renunciation of sexual activity in his conversion, he did not agree with Plotinus in seeing matter and physicality as the prime root of evil. Again, unlike Plotinus (following Plato, *Republic* 509B), Augustine would not say that God should be described as the One 'beyond being'. The Platonic antithesis of the one and the many he could accept as an account of the relation between the transcendent Creator and the manifold diversity of creation. But the one God is never beyond being. Exodus 3: 14 assured him that God is being itself, *ipsum esse*: that which truly is is he. (Two excited and stirring sermons delivered at Hippo to his congregation of dockers and farm-workers developed this remarkable theme: P 134 and Jo 38.9).

Creation is 'participation' in being. This term implies derivation. It is characteristic of that which is derived, that what one has is then distinct from what one is. For creatures it is one thing to exist, another to be just and wise. But in God to exist and to be just, good, and wise are one and the same. Man can exist without being just, good, or wise; God cannot. God 'is what he has'. Plotinus had expressed the same point in Aristotelian terms: in the divine 'substance' (i.e. metaphysical essence) there can be no accidents. Plotinus and Augustine concurred that only the first of the ten categories, substance, is applicable to God's being (C iv.28).

Augustine found the prologue to St John's gospel (a piece of the New Testament that impressed Neoplatonic philosophers) a noble statement of the Platonic world-picture, and of the light of God shining into the darkness to turn the alienated world back towards the higher realms. But in finding Christianity to express the truth so nearly Platonic, Augustine noted one dramatic point of difference: 'the books of the Platonists' did not say the Word was made flesh. The concept of a unique revelation within a particular life was a Christian theme which Mani had had to alter radically. For a pagan Platonist its particularity seemed scandalously incompatible with divine immutability and with a universal operation of providence in the cosmos as a whole. Platonists did not think of a divine purpose

31

being worked out in and through the mess of history, and their conceptions of time were cyclic, not linear; in other words, at immense intervals of time the configuration of the stars would come round to the same position, and then all things would start again on the same treadmill. The concept of a unique incarnation calling man to an existential decision with eternal consequences meant that Platonism was not something Augustine could leave unamended. On the other hand, he too felt it necessary to interpret the incarnation in terms of God's universal providence, as a momentous step towards the goal of history and a clue to its meaning.

At the time of his conversion Augustine was nearly 33, already established as a master of literature and rhetorical style. Had he gone on to the secular career of which he dreamed, little more than his name might have been known to posterity, perhaps only as a striking instance of social mobility on the part of a clever young man from a relatively impecunious provincial family in the Numidian countryside, who had worked hard, and had the luck to enjoy some useful patronage. Now he had renounced that. He had to work out the answers to pressing problems. His first literary undertaking was to inquire into the thorny questions about evil and providence once forced on his attention by the Manichees. He also had to settle accounts with the sceptical thinkers who, during a momentous period, had been deeply congenial to his mind.

During the months at Cassiciacum he composed a series of philosophical dialogues, often modelled on those by Cicero written in his retirement at Tusculum. The literary convention of the dialogue form enabled him to state difficulties with which he himself was still wrestling, and which he could discuss with a thoughtful élite. The atmosphere was that of a lecture-room, using dialectical dispute as a means of instruction, posing problems and seeking solutions. The subjects were, first, the nature of happiness (*De beata vita*), a critique of the sceptical theory of knowledge and the doctrine of suspense of judgement (*Contra Academicos*), and the affirmation that a personal or particular providence is possible within the consistent order of the universe and the chain of cause and effect (*De ordine*). In the last of these he included a defence of the study of the liberal arts as preparing the mind for higher truths, and suggested that they should be arranged in a ladder of ascent, with geometry and music particularly disclosing the mathematical order underlying the cosmos. Augustine borrowed an image from Plotinus and used the illustration of a mosaic pavement whose beauty is not seen by the eye that concentrates on one small piece, but only by the eye that tries to take in the whole. In one very Neoplatonic passage he declared that 'to see the One we must withdraw from plurality not only of men but from sense-perceptions; we seek as it were the centre of the circle which holds the whole together' (O i.3).

At Cassiciacum he also wrote *Soliloquies* (Augustine coined this word), a dialogue in which, in search of certitude especially on the immortality of the soul, he humbly submitted himself to instruction by Reason. A characteristically Neoplatonizing piece of dialectic led him to assert that because mathematical truth is timelessly true, the mind which knows it also shares in this transcendence of the space-time continuum—a view briefly adumbrated in Plato (*Meno* 86A) and then developed considerably by Plotinus (iv.7). In a rich medley of phrases borrowed from Cicero, the *Soliloquies* fuse biblical language with a potent mix of the Neoplatonic ontology. Emphatic reference is made by name to both Plato and Plotinus, and the presence of themes derived from Porphyry is very probable. For Augustine here says that to attain the vision of God there is no single road; but at least one must flee everything physical; set aside the quest for fulfilment whether in sexual love 'even with a modest, well-educated wife', or in wealth and honour; train one's mind to invisible realities by a process analogous to geometrical abstraction, so that one thinks not of squares of varying sizes but of the principles by which all squares have squareness. Then one may begin to comprehend the mysterious transcendence of God, in whom the purified immortal soul finds its true end. The path of inner purification is by faith. The last proposition is the only one that would have puzzled Porphyry.

The Cassiciacum dialogues join confidence that a providential order exists with diffidence about human ability to discern it in all cases. Trust in providence is seen as more than an intellectual puzzle: 'Vision will be granted to him who lives well, prays well, and studies well' (O ii.51). But it is suggested that amid all the diversities and tensions of experience, there can be an ultimate harmony, a beauty found in antitheses and contrasts as in a painted picture where there is light and dark. So also unity of truth may lie beyond the various subjects of human knowledge with their different methods of investigation.

With this significant place assigned to the study of the liberal arts, it was natural for Augustine, in the early days following his baptism, to embark on a series of handbooks to the basic topics of the ancient educational syllabus. Of these textbooks only his books on logic and on music have certainly survived intact. His Grammar, a copy of which lay before Cassiodorus in the sixth century, was found so useful that the copy in his own library was stolen. Medieval manuscripts transmit two grammars under Augustine's name, and it is very possible that one of them (known as the *Ars breviata*) is the 'lost' text. The conclusion is evident that conversion and baptism did nothing to crush the pedagogic and humanist instinct. The Neoplatonic influences set him on the way to seeing the liberal arts (especially dialectic, geometry, and music) as a highly desirable mental training in abstract thought preparatory to higher metaphysical explorations.

At the end of his life Augustine wrote a conscientious critique of his own life-work, the 'Revisions' or 'Reconsiderations' (*Retractationes*, not to be translated 'retractions', for the book is almost as much a positive defence as a withdrawal of indiscretions). In this book he felt that as a young man he had tended to exaggerate the value and importance of such liberal studies: 'Many holy people have not studied them at all, and many who have studied them are not holy' (R i.3.2).

Augustine's educational concern came to find different expression in his maturity, specially in one of his most influential books, the first to be printed in the fifteenth century. This was entitled *De doctrina christiana*, or 'On Christian culture'. He revised and added to it near the end of his life. One manuscript of the first edition, written during Augustine's lifetime, is preserved—now at Leningrad. The work is an examination of the skills needed to interpret the Bible correctly and persuasively. Augustine made use of the *Book of Rules* of the schismatic theologian Tyconius (below, p.55) to formulate canons of exegesis which would avoid subjectivity, e.g. in deciding what is literal, what allegorical and, if the latter, what the hidden meaning is. The Bible disclosed indeed the very wisdom of God; but human science was far from irrelevant to its discovery and elucidation. Vast and dangerous errors were made by interpreters of scripture confident of their own private inspiration. Augustine records with some astonishment that there were contemporary Christians in Africa who read no book other than the Bible, and who conversed in the often strange translationese of the old Latin Bible; an anticipation of Quaker English. He was sure that wider studies were necessary. A biblical scholar needed to know some history, geography, natural science, mathematics, logic, and rhetoric (how to write and speak clearly and appropriately). There could be places where a little knowledge of technology might well help the interpreter. Certainly some knowledge of Greek was most valuable for checking translations and variant readings.

Hebrew Augustine never studied, though he understood words of Punic spoken by the peasants and well knew that it was a cognate Semitic language. He was relieved of the obligation to study Hebrew partly by the thoroughness with which his senior contemporary and pen-friend Jerome had mastered it, partly because he was convinced that the Greek translation of the Old Testament made by the Seventy (Septuagint) was no less inspired than the Hebrew original. Jerome's New Latin Bible (the Vulgate) distressed him when long-familiar words were needlessly altered. It upset the laity, always hostile to liturgical changes.

The tract on Christian culture reflected the special reverence with which Augustine regarded the Bible. He expressly denied that holy scripture represented the sole medium of divine revelation (S 12.4); but it represented the principle of authority which seemed central to Christian belief in a divinely given way of salvation for an ignorant and lost humanity. The authority of Bible and Church rested on reciprocal support. Usage in the churches had determined the limits of the canon. Bible texts established the divinely constituted nature of the Church.

Controversy against Manichee critics made Augustine insist on an inner spiritual meaning, especially of the Old Testament. 'The meaning of the New Testament lies hidden in the Old, the meaning of the Old Testament is revealed through the New' (CR iv.8). So Christ's coming fulfilled the aspiration of the Old Testament prophets. Manichees made him very conscious of the dividing line between the books accepted as canonical by the Church and the apocryphal Gospels and Acts to which Mani had often appealed, especially because these apocrypha were written to foster the view that marriage is out of the question for a believer. The Manichee contention that the New Testament text had been corrupted in transmission made him aware of the importance of variant readings among the manuscripts, or of errors in the Old Latin Bible. He did not understand the biblical text to bear only one sense intended at the time by the original author. The biblical writers themselves frequently used symbolism and allegory. To insist on a single literal and historical sense must mean failure to grasp the underlying message.

In a few places Augustine could write confidently of the clarity and perspicuity of the Bible. But there are other places where he had to allow that many texts are obscure, and that not everything necessary to salvation is obvious to any and every casual reader. This is reinforced by the observation that many heretics start from a mistaken or partisan interpretation of scripture and, because they are both clever and proud, are reluctant to correct themselves. 'It is part of a catholic disposition to express the wish to accept correction if one is mistaken' (DEP ii.5).

5

If one finds the PRINCIPAL in the text, then one finds lasting meaning beyond historical event

3 Free choice

In the summer of 387, living with Monica at Rome during what was to be the last year of her life, Augustine began a substantial and complex treatise 'on the origin of evil and on free choice' (*De libero arbitrio*), a work which he finally completed six or seven years later. The critique of Manichee dualism and determinism led him to lay strong emphasis on the will. That it had a central position in every ethical action he demonstrated by appealing to the cardinal virtues of justice, prudence, self-control, and courage. Virtue depends on right and rational choices, and therefore happiness lies in loving goodness of will. By contrast, misery is the product of an evil will. And evil originated in a misused free choice which neglected eternal goodness, beauty, and truth.

We have seen that Augustine preferred to locate the root of evil in the soul's instability rather than, with Plotinus, in the body and in matter (CD xiv.3). The soul's weakness was for him the immediate, if not necessarily the all-sufficient, cause of sin. Yet he saw this instability of the soul as inherent in the very fact of being created out of nothing and therefore 'contingent', liable to be driven off course. Even its immortality it possesses not by its own inherent nature but by the gift and will of the Creator.

Creation out of nothing carried for Augustine the consequence that in everything so created there is an element of non-being and a 'tendency to non-existence', even though that ultimate stage is never actually reached. By using such language he sought to hold together a biblical concept of the createdness and dependence of the soul with a Platonic assertion of the soul's immortality. In an early essay on *The Immortality of the Soul* (a work containing numerous passages echoing Porphyry), he wrote that if even the matter of the body is not annihilated at death, so also the sinful soul retains for ever some trace of the divine image and form. In his maturity he would write that 'even the fallen soul remains God's image' (T xiv.4), 'capable of knowing God' (*capax Dei*, xiv.11). For 'even irreligious people' think about eternity by implication, as when they make assertive moral judgements on the behaviour of others ignoring the fact that they behave none too well themselves (xiv.21). So even in the worst cases, the soul retains the marks of rationality and freedom which are the meaning of 'the image of God' bestowed on man by creation. At the same time, being created out of nothing, it is mutable, and the potentiality for the fall is therefore given by creation. Even so the actual choice of the will to neglect the good is causeless and inexplicable.

The dilemma here long troubled his mind. Why, he asked, did some angels fall while others did not? In his maturity it seemed to him inadequate to speak about random chance and causelessness. To meet the difficulty he turned to a doctrine of predestination.

Although Augustine dissented from Plotinus' opinion that evil begins in matter, he agreed that the prime consequence of the soul's mistaken choice is that it has become obsessively attached to the body. Matter in itself is morally neutral; yet merely by the fact of being created out of nothing, by being in itself formless, it carries a profound metaphysical inferiority. Even so, the soul is the real field of battle. The 'nature' with which humanity is endowed by the Creator is good; Adam before the Fall and Christ in his incarnation have 'pure nature' such as the rest of humanity cannot have now. For the corruption of weak choices results in a chain of habit being formed, which fetters the character and becomes second nature, flawed or 'vitiated' nature.

Experience in moral decisions shows that we are ignorant of just what is right and moreover, when we do know, have great difficulty in performing it. Augustine felt hesitation on the question whether 'ignorance and difficulty' are part of God's initial design for his creatures, to teach them as they mature gradually to master their problems and stand on their own feet; or whether the moral struggle is a permanent and penal consequence of the fallen estate of man since Adam's and Eve's first disobedience. Augustine could afford to be hesitant at this point, since, for the argument of his treatise on freedom of choice, it mattered relatively little. Later he became more inclined to the penal view. But in the earlier work his objective was simply to refute the Manichee contention that the evils of human life prove the created world not to be the work of supreme goodness and unopposed power. He was aware that he was leaving a number of questions unresolved.

The treatise on free choice was later hailed by critics of Augustine who followed Pelagius (below, p. 108) in the conviction that the late Augustine failed to do justice to freedom and therefore took moral value out of acts of virtue. The critics liked to quote the treatise as containing arguments for free will unrefuted even by their author. He could reply with good reason that the attempt to play the young Augustine off against the old was ill founded. He admitted that there were some few sentences which he could have worded more precisely. He felt the book was better on sin than on grace. The argument of the treatise included an insistence on the transmission to posterity of Adam's guilt and penalty, on the impotence of sinful man to rescue himself by effort of will, and on the need for the humility of the Redeemer to conquer the pride and envy which constitute the most diabolical features of the Fall.

The second of the three parts of the treatise on free choice contains Augustine's most considerable and sustained statement of the argument for assenting to the existence of God. Characteristically he approached the problem as a central issue in the theory of knowledge. He did not undertake to prove God's existence as if he were demonstrating the existence of an object in the world of sense. His argument is not that the sum total of things includes God in the way in which it includes things perceived by the mind through the five physical senses. He understood God to be beyond time and space, for within time and space man cannot discover an ultimate happiness or perfection. Similarly God is presupposed by all thought about universals and by communication between minds. Mathematical, aesthetic, and moral reasoning takes it for granted that there is a realm of reality beyond the senses. (Physical objects can be perceived; physical theory cannot, and yet has to be formulated in language taken from the realm of sense-objects. A person who denied the truth of the fundamentals of physics would be thought strange; it is no serious objection that language about these fundamentals is largely analogical.)

Therefore if we question the wonderful order of nature with its noble objects, in reason's ear they declare 'The hand that made us is divine' (C ix.25; xi.6; quoting Plotinus iii.2.3,20). But the order, design, beauty, even the very mutability and flux of the world and the fact that its existence is not 'necessary', become no more than subordinate and supporting considerations in the argument. The essence of the matter appears in Augustine's conviction that God is not just someone or something who happens to exist; he is Being itself, and the source of all finite beings. As a good Platonist he finds this assured by the reality of the moral principles, justice, wisdom, truth. They stand supreme in the scale of value; yet they are realities no one has seen, touched, tasted, smelt, or heard.

Not that Augustine would disparage the importance of the senses. Their evidence is fundamental for all things that fall within their range. Questions of taste, colour, softness, size, shape, etc., we decide by the relevant senses. But the perceptions of the senses are a low form of apprehension. The sceptical philosophers rightly warned that the senses can be deceptive, as an oar in the water appears crooked. The information derived through the senses is checked and judged by the perceiving, knowing mind.

Augustine liked a formula which he found in Plotinus and which in turn Plotinus took from Plato's *Philebus*, namely that when the body receives sensation, the soul 'is not unaware' of the fact. The supremacy of the soul is implicit. There is, however, a gulf between the perpetual flux and change of the realm of the five senses and the timeless truths of mathematics and universals.

In Augustine's hands the argument about God's existence merges into the argument of the Platonists for the reality of universals as eternal and immutable truths, whether these be of mathematics or of transcendent values of justice and truth, in the light of which the mind judges whether a particular act or proposition is just or true. For him the crux is that there is a realm of reality, beyond and above the mind of man which is itself mutable and seldom continues long in one stay. We are again seeing the imprint of the conviction born of the mystical experience described in the seventh book of the *Confessions*, through which he was confronted by the antithesis between his own impermanence and the eternal changelessness of the God who is (above, p. 23).

Accordingly he saw the goal of his inferences in the notion of unchanging, eternal, necessary being. Naturally he was well aware that the goal was given for him by faith. No seeker after truth begins with no convictions about where and how it may be found. Faith is always prior in time to understanding. But the understanding remains a matter of reasoning and philosophical inference. 'Believe in order that you may understand', he liked to quote (from the Old Latin Bible version of Isaiah). But for Augustine the relationship between faith and reason is not what it later became for the medieval schoolmen. The propositions of faith which the understanding seeks to interpret turn out to be matters not of revelation, but of what medieval theologians would have called 'natural theology'; matters (that is) established by philosophical argument without accepting any claim to a specific revelation. In the treatise on free choice Augustine seeks to argue that it is reasonable to accept belief in God, immortality, freedom, and moral responsibility—beliefs which Platonic philosophers knew and shared without having a Bible to help them.

The treatises written by Augustine in his thirties have many references to the question of immortality, including the rather obscure essay in Neoplatonizing dialectic concerning *The Immortality of the Soul* (a work which he himself did not rate highly when he re-read it later in life). Death was often present to his consciousness, especially when friends or young people were carried off by sickness. Human life he described as a race towards death (CD 13.10); and 'one should begin each day not with complacency that one has survived another day but with compunction that one more day of one's allotted span has for ever passed'. Finally, his conviction that death is not the end rested not on Platonic dialectic but on faith in the risen Christ (T xiii.12).

4   A philosophical society

By the late autumn of 388, after Monica's requiem at Ostia, Augustine had returned to his native Africa (which he was never again to leave) and settled at his home town, Thagaste, to practise an experiment in ascetic retirement with Alypius and other friends. The lay community met regularly for daily prayers and the recitation of the Psalter. (It is hard to exaggerate the importance of the Psalter for Augustine's spirituality; psalm-quotations have been shown to be essential to the very structure of the *Confessions*.) In between their hours of devotion they discussed Cicero, St Paul, and Neoplatonic themes. The community was quietist, contemplative in spirit, and rather donnish, with Augustine as acknowledged leader providing answers to questions raised in the discussions. These answers circulated in writing and were later collected to make a notable book, *On 83 different questions*. The 46th contains an important statement about Plato's theory of Ideas, safeguarding biblical monotheism by holding that universals are 'thoughts in the mind of God'. The Thagaste community was not called a monastery. The 'society of brothers', as they were called, shared property, lived in frugal simplicity, but had no formal vows, no identical clothing, no fixed rule and requirement of obedience. They were far more intellectual than most later monasteries. Nevertheless the community had the thing, if not the name, and was in practice the first monastic community in Latin Africa.

In this lay community Augustine lived for two and a half years; it was a fruitful period for his writing. The gradual transition from teaching the liberal arts to serious engagement with theology was marked by his six books *On Music*. Five of the six books were devoted to a technical discussion of metre and rhythm. He intended later to continue his studies with a discussion of the theoretical aspects of pitch, but this was never written, and that field was left open for Boethius 120 years later. (Practical music-making was no proper pursuit for an intellectual and a gentleman in antiquity; that was left to vulgar people and girls hired to entertain the gentlemen after dinner.)

The sixth book on Music is of a different character, and enjoyed some independent circulation. It was Augustine's restatement of Plato's belief that mathematical principles underlie everything in the universe and are the principal clues to its providential ordering. Especially in the *Timaeus* Plato had taught that the very structure of the soul is determined by ratios directly related to the ratios of intervals in music; e.g. an octave is 2 to 1, a fifth 3 to 2, a fourth 4 to 3, a whole tone 9 to 8. Indeed the same ratios governed the distances between the planets.

Augustine mentions more than once that he was vulnerable to being moved by the sound of music. At Milan, where at first he used to come to the cathedral to admire Ambrose's oratorical skill, he found himself not only impressed by the content of the discourses but also gripped by the psalm chants. He knew that fitting music is capable of bringing the meaning of words home to the heart. When he was a young man he found music indispensable to his life as a source of consolation. In his maturity there was little time for that anyway, but he remained persuaded by Plato's thesis that between music and the soul there is a 'hidden affinity', *occulta familiaritas* (C x.49). No other art is equally independent of at least four of the five senses, and so controlled by mathematical principles. What power of the mind is more astonishing than its ability to recall music without actually hearing any physical sounds? The observation seemed to Augustine a striking demonstration of the soul's transcendence in relation to the body.

The study of Plotinus' analysis of the nature of beauty (i.6) made a deep impact. Augustine was struck by the per-

45

vasiveness of mathematical order in the cosmos, and this had been a prominent theme in the Cassiciacum dialogues. There his vindication of providence is in substance aesthetic and Plotinian: i.e. the chiaroscuro of light and dark contribute to the beauty of the whole. But this beauty is not merely a subjective feeling; it is grounded in numbers. There is precision not only in the inanimate environment, but also in the processes of human life, as is obvious from the study of embryology which shows how the embryo reaches each successive stage of development at constant and exact intervals of time. Moreover, Augustine added, the beauty of a building depends on its mathematical proportions. Symmetry of fenestration depends on measurements. So beauty has an objective ground. Things please the eye because they are beautiful, not merely vice versa. (This was a judgement he would qualify only in part when speaking of a man's love for a woman. While the symmetry and proportion of the human body were indeed measurable in mathematical terms, Augustine added, with what may seem to the modern reader extraordinary romanticism, 'Adam did not love Eve because she was beautiful; it was his love which made her beautiful': P 132.10.)

In some texts we meet the normal Neoplatonic view that mathematics is a halfway house in the ascent from the physical world to metaphysics and theology. He had to warn his readers against taking him to mean that pure mathematics is metaphysics without qualification. One should not suppose that geometry is a particularly obscure way of talking theology (Sol. i.11). In any event, he drily remarks, not more than a handful of the clever mathematicians known to him could actually be called 'wise' (LA ii.30).

Augustine wanted to ask not merely why the world is there at all, but also how our minds can know things both through the five senses and through words which are 'signs'. Analytical questions about the function of language need first to be asked if one is to go on to the existential questions which lie beyond them. This concern for words and meanings and their relation to reality was stimulated by his growing role as a lay theologian interpreting a divine self-disclosure through 'the word of God'. He was highly sensitive to the fact that much religious language is figurative and indirect: what unreflecting people, whether believers or unbelievers, may take as plain matter-of-fact prose is often a pile of imaginative metaphors enshrining profound intuition and insight rather than representing the conclusion of reasoned inference. He was aware that religious aspiration can have, at least for many, a close affinity with music. During his lifetime the Catholic churches of North Africa were increasingly coming to terms with pictorial art and were installing murals portraying Christ, Mary, Peter and Paul, or Old Testament saints— Adam and Eve (decently covered), the sacrifice of Isaac, and others. The Platonist in him felt reserve towards the power of art to come between the soul and God rather than always to act as a bridge from sense to spirit. But he defended church music against puritans who wanted to exclude it altogether, and acknowledged that, dangerous as music may be, it is a natural medium for emotions of exaltation and awed abasement.

As a layman at Thagaste Augustine also wrote two of his most effective works, 'The Teacher' (*de magistro*) and 'True Religion' (*de vera religione*).

'The Teacher' was written as a memorial to his clever natural son Adeodatus, in conversation with whom the ideas were worked out. It concerns how human beings can communicate truth. The discussion begins with the simple answer that we do this by words. But then that naïve answer is brought increasingly under the fire of criticism. Words are sounds significant by convention, but convey meaning only in an ambivalent and limited degree. The meaning of an utterance is at least as much determined by the tone of voice or the context or gestures as by the syllables pronounced. The facial expression of the speaker will disclose to members of his own circle if he is being ironical. Some idiomatic phrases can bear a sense which is the opposite of what the words appear to say. To describe a man as an honest lawyer indeed may not mean just what it says. Moreover, words can be used as a smokescreen, to conceal or to deceive, to impart disinformation. In any event, words are mere physical sounds. It is mind that gives them significance.

Certainly Augustine was the last person to deny that words are useful. So great a master of their employment was unlikely to think they played no part. Moreover, the Bible uses words; and sacraments are 'visible words' (F 19.16), for it is the Word and Spirit which impart power and inward meaning to what would otherwise be only an external ceremonial act (Jo 80.3). But it does not follow that words can in themselves be effective or adequate for conveying full meaning in matters of great weight. Truth is ultimately communicated through an intangible, inaudible, indescribable experience of the interaction of mind with mind. For mind can be known only by mind.

This thesis led Augustine to reflect on the nature of prayer. Minds of close friends can communicate with one another without a word being uttered, perhaps with not even a gesture. The God who is incomprehensible and transcendent is also more 'interior' than anything we can express. 'When we pray, often we can hardly know the meaning of the words we are using' (Sol. i.9). This inadequacy is partly inherent in the fact that our terms and categories belong to discourse taken from this world of space, time, and successiveness. They therefore blur and distort the truth about the immutable and eternal. Partly it is a mark of all matters involving deep feeling (and no word became more characteristic of Augustine than 'longing', *desiderium*) that they lie too deep for words. 'Man can say nothing of what he is incapable of feeling, but he can feel what he is incapable of putting into words' (S 117.7f.; P 99.5).

The ultimate power of mutual understanding between friends, he believed, rested on a common participation in the divine Reason. This belief cohered with his exalted, sometimes emotional language about the gift of friendship. To share in the light radiating from Christ the Teacher is to be enabled to recognize the identical faith in others. Augustine sometimes spoke of the religious community as having a capacity, through an indefinable intuition, to discern authentic and inauthentic forms of the faith. 'Catholic ears', he thought, did not normally need formal decisions by synods to tell them the fundamentals of their faith (DEP iv.36). This illumination of the mind, then, is a power or sense of discretion rather than information about the facts. It penetrates the profounder levels of the personality. Introspection taught Augustine the existence of the sub-conscious: 'You can know something which you are not aware that you know' (T xiv.9).

Admittedly, there is another series of texts in which he wrote of the impenetrable depths of the human heart, of the 'abyss' of man. 'Every heart is closed to every heart' (P 55.9). To God every motive is known, but not to man (134.16). Man himself is an ocean depth, *grande profundum* (C iv.22), and the individual cannot even comprehend his own character and heart (P 41.13).

He had a more than ordinary interest in logical tangles. But his interest in what a modern reader would think of as depth psychology helped to make him sceptical of ingenious language-games played by clever dialecticians. Their doctrine 'lacked heart' (C ix.1 and elsewhere). Valuable as a training in logic was in his view (for theologians he thought it indispensable), religion engaged yet deeper levels of the personality. Religious truth he spoke of as an inner illumination from 'God the sun of souls'. He never suggested that true ideas are inherent or innate within the soul. They always appear as the Creator's gift.

By the term 'soul' (*anima*) Augustine meant the highest immaterial element in man, the part of man to which the

49

mind (*mens*, more rarely *animus*) is but a function. Exactly what 'soul' is and how God creates souls he regarded as beyond human knowledge. It would make for simplicity, he once remarked apropos of infant baptism (GL x.19), if all Adam's posterity derived souls as well as bodies from their first parent by heredity. But this doctrine (traducianism) that souls are acquired by heredity carried more physical implications than at least some Platonists could feel at ease with. Perhaps it would be preferable to say that God expressly creates a soul for each individual as conceived. (Augustine ignored as silly the objection that the Creator should be spared endless fuss.) Or, more platonically, all souls exist in God from the first, and are either sent or even choose to come and inhabit bodies on earth. Neoplatonic philosophers were disagreed among themselves on the correct answer, and the Bible offered no guidance. In Augustine's mind none of these options could be finally excluded. His refusal to give a decision incurred sharp criticism from some who felt that such a question simply could not be left in the limbo of indecision. He remained unmoved.

Diffidence about the capacity of finite minds to comprehend the infinite and eternal led him to use strongly relativist language about the God who is beyond our knowing. Commenting on the prologue to St John's Gospel he wrote that 'Because John was inspired he was able to say something. Had he not been inspired, he would have said nothing at all.' Even the acceptance of a divine revelation mediated through the Bible left unqualified the proposition that this is accommodated to the modest capacity of the recipient and expressed in images (C xiii.18–19). In one stark sentence he declared that the concept must be less than adequate to God 'if you can comprehend it' (S 117.5), or, in a paradox, 'it is better to find God by not finding him [i.e. by learning that he is beyond your grasp] than by finding not to find him'. (C i.10). The causality of grace is always beyond human grasp (SL 7). Nevertheless the

massive agnosticism of such sayings did not decline into
scepticism, and he knew that there are degrees of
inadequacy.

Augustine confronted the Academics sceptical of the
possibility of certainty as a man who had once been one of
them. They liked to say that one could never attain truth,
only probability or an approximation, something like the
truth. He thought that if a proposition could be said to
resemble the truth, there must be truth which one is judging it to resemble. He also attached emphatic weight to an
argument which he often repeated and which, in another
context, became important to Descartes in the seventeenth
century: '*I think, therefore I am*; even if I am mistaken,
nevertheless I am.' A person who doubts must at least be
utterly confident of his own existence, or he would not be
in a position to doubt. Suspense of judgement is therefore
not a watertight or rational position.

In passing, we may notice that, unlike Descartes,
Augustine did not argue that certitude is found exclusively
in the subjective state of the doubting mind. He did not
need, as Descartes did, to make his *Cogito* the sole foundation of knowledge. But it is true that he regarded the pure
truths of mathematics as incomparably more certain than
any perceptions of the five senses.

Augustine pushed the argument further, in a Platonic
direction, to imply that there is a capacity in the mind to
know truths in a way far more significant than the stream
of sensations and perceptions coming through the body. If
something, then, is indubitable, there really are truths to be
known. The mind hungers for truth; no one can bear to be
deceived (C x.34; S 306.9; DDC i.40). None can be happy
if he greatly desires but cannot attain the truth. But this last
proposition is modified by Augustine under the pressure of
a religious consideration: in religious truth, knowledge is
not a static possession of the knower, but an ever-growing
relationship to God. Every person who seeks truth has God
beside him to help, and that suffices for happiness even

51

without the full grasp of the truth sought (BV 20). The enjoyment of God is an 'insatiable satisfaction' (S 362.28). In a number of texts Augustine constructs a ladder of ascent with seven stages of the soul's progress in maturity of comprehension (VR 49; QA 70–6; DDC ii.7).

He did not think there is knowledge in which the knowing mind does not play a large role. On the one hand, nothing is known unless there is an inward desire of the mind moving it to desire understanding. We cannot love that of which nothing is known. But that axiom presupposes that one already has an inkling about the subject arousing one's curiosity. 'It is an important element in discovery to ask the right question and to know what it is you wish to find out' (QH prol.). He used Platonic language about the educational process; it is an evoking of a capacity, in some sense a knowledge, which is already present.

He shared Plotinus' dislike of the notion that the object known is so wholly distinct from and external to the knowing subject that in the act of knowing there is no significant personal element. An element of self-consciousness attaches to our knowledge of the external world, and the personal subject is not to be eliminated. If you know something, you also know that it is you who know. So the theme that understanding requires love to attain its end merges by this route into theology. He put it in this way: all inquiry about how we can know God comes back to the question 'what do we understand by love?' (T viii.10). The Creator's love is immanent within the mind and will of his rational creatures (T viii.12). 'We move towards God not by walking but by loving' (*non ambulando, sed amando*). 'Not our feet but our moral character carries us nearer to him. Moral character is assessed not by what a man knows but by what he loves' (E 155.13).

Hence the negative path, which surrounds the idea of God with exclusively negative epithets, is not the only way. Certainly we can more easily say what God is not than what he is (P 85.23). But at least our ignorance is informed, *docta ignorantia* (E 130.28). The believer's language oscillates between confidence and diffidence. Here Augustine made his own a paradox he found in Porphyry. The contemplation of God is an experience beyond intellection, and 'somehow such things are known by a not knowing, and so by this kind of knowing their mysteriousness is realized' (CD xii.7; C xii.5).

'On True Religion' was composed for Romanianus, the wealthy landowner of Thagaste who had once financed his education, and had been converted to Manicheism by the clever young Augustine. Augustine had to unconvert him and bring him to Catholicism. The treatise has an anti-Manichee thrust, but is chiefly remarkable for the presence of Neoplatonic themes within a strongly Christian and Catholic framework. His appeal was to the uniqueness of the one Church, the 'catholica' which even rival sects would recognize as such ('ask them where the Catholic church is in a town, and even they will not have the nerve to direct you to their own conventicle'). The title-deeds of this one Church lie in a sacred history recorded in holy scripture. Its doctrines are then vindicated by their coherence with reason (meaning Platonism).

The coherence of faith and reason Augustine saw in the fact that if concessions to polytheistic rites were removed from Platonism, this philosophy came so close to Christianity that 'with the change of a few words and opinions many Platonists have become Christians' (VR 7). The Neoplatonists' notion of the hierarchy of being and their vindication of providence could be given systematic integration into a Christian framework, and the aspiration of the Platonic tradition was that which Christ had made possible. The content of salvation is then defined as happiness, the inner security which comes as the soul turns away from pride, passion, and the multiplicity of distractions, and ascends towards the One, towards pure reason, to the God who is met in the humility of Christ. Augustine saw Christ as able to bring redemption because in one person he is both God and man. The God–Man is the way and the ladder by which God enables us to rise from the temporal to the eternal. He is both road and goal, Jacob's ladder. By knowing the Son of Man in history, we may come to discern the eternal wisdom of God (T xiii.24). He is both example and gift, our pattern and our expiation; the Mediator for whom Porphyry had no room, though he fitted in a large number of other inferior mediators. At first believers begin with the example of Christ the man, who is 'the milk of babes'; but Christ raises to his own true level all who obey and trust in him (C vii.20). Several texts of Augustine boldly describe salvation as 'deification', language commoner in the Greek than in the Latin theologians of antiquity. But the language is often qualified: 'it is one thing to be God, another to participate in God' (CD xxii.30,3). We cannot be sure that 'in the next life we shall be changed into God's substance and become what he is, as some say' (N 37). What is meant is that we are 'united to God by love' (M i.20).

Some contemporaries of Augustine who had lost all belief in the old gods sought no replacement by looking towards Christianity. He described them as dismissing all religion as enslaving superstition. They wished to assert the freedom and sovereignty of the individual as master of his own soul in sailing the sea of faith. Augustine's comment (more unkind than untrue perhaps) was that the assertion of splendid autonomy would be more impressive if those who claimed to have shuffled off the fetters of all religion were not found to end up in bondage. Their egocentric enslavement might be to bodily pleasure and comfort, or to naked ambition for power and wealth or, in the case of the intelligentsia, to an endless quest for a this-worldly knowledge which could never hope to be more than relative and tended to dilettantism. (Platonism, which did not much encourage Augustine to be interested in natural science, also influenced him against the Aristotelian notion that knowledge may be sought for its own sake. He took it to be self-evident that the prime tasks of philosophy lie in logic and ethics.) 'Man is slave to that by which he wishes to find happiness' (VR 69). The longing for authentic happiness is the point at which man discovers God within. (One notes here the fusion of the *Hortensius* with Porphyry.) 'Do not go outside yourself', even by looking at the external world with its mathematical perfection; but return into your own personality. The mind is a mirror reflecting divine truth; but it is mutable. Therefore 'transcend yourself' and seek the unchanging and eternal ground of all being. Then you will find that 'the service of God is perfect freedom' (VR 87).

The tract's appeal to what is universal in nature and in reason is crossed by a very different theme, namely the affirmation of a divine purpose in history. This is summed up in the biblical antitheses between the wheat and the tares, the old man and the new, outward and inward. There are 'two kinds of people'. This duality speaks of the mysterious presence, in an alienated and secular society, of a hidden people of God. In this way the Platonic contrast between sense and mind became fused with a major theme taken ultimately from biblical Apocalyptic. This passage (VR 49–50) is the earliest occurrence of a theme which he would later come to orchestrate for full brass. Ten years later the two kinds of people have become 'two loves', two cities, Babylon and Jerusalem. More than twenty years later the doctrine of the two cities became the foundation of one of his greatest works, the *City of God*.

There has been scholarly controversy about the source or impetus which made this notion important to Augustine. Was it a residuum of Manichee dualism with its cosmic conflict of Light and Dark, of God and the prince of darkness? An alternative which has seemed much more plausible to most scholars is the deep impression made on Augustine by Tyconius, a theologian of the schismatic Donatists who dissented from his colleagues in holding that the true Church must be universal. His opinions brought him so close to the hated Catholics that he was excommunicated. He did not join the Catholic community for reasons that can only be conjectured—e.g. that a shift of individual allegiance could hinder corporate *rapprochement*. Tyconius' wrote an extant *Book of Rules* for interpreting scripture, and a commentary on the Apocalypse of John, the surviving fragments of which show that the contrast of the two cities of Babylon and Jerusalem was important to him.

A strong interest in the Apocalypse of John was not, however, confined to the Donatist schismatics. It was common to African Christians generally.

5 Vocation

In the lay society at Thagaste Augustine did not find that he had solved his problems. At one stage he seriously considered withdrawal to desert solitude. But that was never to be. Early in 391, on a visit to the port of Hippo Regius 45 miles from Thagaste, he was forcibly ordained presbyter for the small Catholic congregation. (Most Christians at Hippo were then of the Donatist persuasion.) His contemplative endeavours were abruptly ended, but he could not refuse. He sat down with his Bible to equip himself for a calling to which he felt unfitted by temperament, inclination, and physical health. He wanted to be a monk, not a busy town parson continually beset by unreasonable people. The old bishop who had ordained him allowed a compromise. In a garden by the Hippo church he built a monastery. There came to live with him a few elderly and retired clergy, but in the main the community consisted of lay brothers who maintained the house either by manual labour or by working as clerks for the merchants on the waterfront. Much less well educated than the lay society at Thagaste, which broke up on Augustine's departure, the Hippo brothers daily chanted the Psalter and biblical canticles. (Hymns with words not in scripture were only sparingly admitted to Catholic practice in Africa—they were a Donatist custom.) Though no formal vow of poverty was required, all surrendered property on entering the house; for most of them it represented greater economic security than they might get outside the walls. Wine was allowed for the sick, meat when guests came. On entry they were formally vested in a monastic habit, and wore a distinctive cap so that they were at once identifiable in the street. They had to become accustomed to being pitied by the crowd who were returning from the music hall or the amphitheatre; Augustine

57

pin-pointed the essence of the matter in the remark that their life could be significant only in the light of otherworldly values (S 46.10). 'He who does not think of the world to come, he who is a Christian for any reason other than that he may receive God's ultimate promises, is not yet a Christian' (S 9.4). Soon there was also a house for nuns of which Augustine's widowed sister became 'mother'.

He found that people brought their old problems with them when they entered the monastery. Experience quickly showed that those with defects of character, with a weakness for drink, with a propensity to avarice or other negative traits, did not leave them behind on making their solemn profession and statement of ascetic resolve. This evoked from Augustine the sad observation that there are crooks in every profession (P 99.13). He had intended his monastery as a battle-school for Christ's front-line soldiers; and many of his monks did go out to serve as bishops. But the Hippo house was also a hospital for some of the more striking misfits and casualties of life.

He composed a Rule for his monastery (E 211) which survives in two distinct lines of transmission, one the edition intended for the sisters in the nunnery, the other a masculine version for the men's house. From the mid eleventh century the latter was taken as a basis for the communities of Austin or Regular Canons, an order which continues to this day. The Rule is remarkably brief, and also noteworthy for its lack of emphasis on penitential motivation. But Augustine was much opposed to excess in mortifications. His ideal for 'Christ's Poor' was contemplative tranquillity with frugality and self-discipline, but not self-hatred, not the suppression of all natural feeling, and never the risking of health.

The rules of discipline were not casually administered. We (once only) hear of corporal punishment being administered to a young monk found chatting with the nuns at an 'unfitting hour'. Augustine's central message was that since we have here no continuing city, let us travel very light. Nevertheless his ideal, like his own personal practice (of which we have an eye-witness description from his contemporary biographer Possidius, who lived with him at Hippo before becoming bishop of the next town, Calama, nearby), has the stamp of deep austerity. He was continually suspicious of the senses as a hindrance to the ascent of the spirit to God, and thought the believer must be continually vigilant against all insidious laxity. Many passages of Augustine warn his readers of the fact that the corrupting and corroding effect of sinful habit begins with 'little things'. In the *Confessions* (ix.18) he even instanced the way in which his mother Monica, when young, had developed a habit of sipping wine in the family cellar until she became almost addicted. Moreover, one sin may lead to another. A serious lie is told to cover a minor peccadillo. A murderer whose crime has been seen by another will have to murder the witness too if he is to escape being found out (P 57.4). Little grains of sand can weigh as much as lead (S 56.12).

The ascetic movement and institutions of the fourth century sprang from one of those profound longings of human aspiration which are much easier to describe than to account for. The ascetic principle is as old as Christianity (Matt. 19: 12; 1 Cor. 7). Moreover, serious philosophers of the classical world spoke with one voice against self-indulgence as a generator of misery, none more eloquently than the theoretical hedonist Epicurus. Stoics had powerfully urged the need to suppress the passions, the desire for wealth and honour and indeed for all transient goods which someone may take away from the holder. In the Platonic tradition the powerful contrast between soul and body as belonging to essentially different worlds encouraged a disparagement of worldly things. Pagan Neoplatonists were hardly less given to austerity than their Christian contemporaries, and had their own holy men, inspired charismatics with powers of moral discernment enhanced by their frugal simplicity of outlook and by their renunciation of marriage.

In comparison with Plotinus and Porphyry, Augustine spoke more positively about the concrete merits of a lay vocation in the world. Lay Christians, he said in his *Questions on the Gospels* (ii.44), can do the things of the secular world and 'keep the wheel of the world's business turning in ways that can be put to the service of God.' He emphatically affirmed that a Christian who had the opportunity to become a magistrate had a duty to do so (CD xix.6).

Nevertheless the rigorism of his ascetic resolve was never relaxed. People who became monks or nuns and then left the monastery for the life over the wall were more than a deep disappointment to him. Ex-monks he thought very unsuitable candidates for holy orders. One widow vowed that if her daughter recovered from her sickbed, the girl would take the veil as a nun. When the girl recovered, the mother asked if her daughter could now be released from any obligation, and if the vow of her own widowhood could be accepted in lieu. Augustine thought that what she had promised should be carried out; i.e. the mother's duty was to persuade her daughter to become a nun. For if the girl did not do so, while she would not thereby exclude herself from the kingdom of heaven, her reward hereafter would certainly be diminished.

Penitence of heart Augustine regarded as part of the regular pattern of all authentic spiritual life. Austere frugality should be voluntarily accepted by believers as a self-imposed discipline (Augustine did not speak of such austerities as imposed formally by the clergy). Intervention by authority was necessary for very serious sins such as adultery, murder, and sacrilege. Of these adultery was far the commonest problem in his flock. It would entail suspension from eucharistic communion and taking one's seat in a special part of the church building reserved for penitents. The absolution and remission of sins is the gift of Christ alone, he taught (T xiii.26); it is Christ who has entrusted to his Church the power of the keys whereby on condition of faith believers may be absolved (DDC i.17).

Penitents were solemnly restored in Holy Week, in the presence of the assembled faithful, in preparation for Easter communion. Augustine mentions pastoral counselling and private rebukes of individual sinners, but no regular system of auricular confession and private absolution which was not pastoral practice in his time. Restored sinners were welcomed back to communion by laying on of hands, and the line of penitents in Holy Week might be 'extremely long' (S 232.8). But these were special cases of serious lapses.

Even the best and holiest of believers, he once declared (CD xix.27), knows that in this life 'our righteousness consists more in the remission of sins than in perfection of virtues'. The baptized believer is both just and a sinner (P 140.14f.; E 185.40). For Augustine this confession of the believer's continual need for pardon was enhanced by his strong sense of the nothingness of the creature before the sublimity of God. Here was language to fire Martin Luther.

Coherent with this spiritual ideal is his ascetic longing to purge the empirical Church of compromises with the world. Some of his most alarming utterances in sermons and letters were addressed to delinquent or weak clergy who fiddled the accounts of the church chest, or who found that their duty of hospitality disclosed in them a fatal weakness for the bottle, or who gave an imprudent hug of consolation to a woman in spiritual distress and found that the relationship did not quite stop there. The duty of administering rebuke cost him much inward pain and strain. But he was sure that those who praised a bishop for being easygoing could only be wicked people (P 128.4). To be approved of for broadmindedness was a sure sign of treachery to one's calling. Augustine spoke with a hesitant voice about secularity within the Church community. On the one hand, he freely acknowledged that no believer attains perfection in this life, and that many are beset by weaknesses and failures. On the other hand, when speaking of 'nominal Christians', baptized perhaps but not visibly admitting the grace of God into their lives, Augustine wrote that they are not authentic believers and should not be counted among God's elect. Similarly the episcopate included very worldly and mediocre men, ambitious for the secular standing and temporal honours, but essentially numbered among the tares to be left until the harvest and then burnt as worthless and injurious.

Dedicated without reservation to the ascetic life, Augustine longed to diffuse it throughout the African churches. He wanted town clergy to live not with their families but together in a clergy house. Naturally he did not expect all Christians to become monks. But he certainly asked 'ordinary' Christians to live highly disciplined lives touched by stern renunciation. Christ had given precepts essential to all followers, but there were also in the gospels 'counsels' or recommendations given to those who would be perfect and aspire to higher things. Missionaries in the African churches, and probably elsewhere, were normally unmarried ascetics living in the utmost simplicity. In a striking phrase Augustine speaks of them as 'fires of holiness and glory' (C xiii.25). But he was much opposed to a contemporary tendency for monks to think of themselves as having a quite separate calling apart from the Church as a whole, as if they were called out of the Church rather than out of the world. He strongly felt that they should never refuse the call to serve as bishops or parish priests where that was what the Church needed them to do. The nuns had a special social role in care for the sick and in rescuing foundlings. In antiquity exposure was a fate to which baby girls were peculiarly liable. But there were also many desperately poor families for whom the arrival of any additional child beyond two or three spelt economic disaster, and who could not be sure of being able to sell off to slave-traders children they could not afford to feed. Foundlings and orphans were a special object of care to bishops, and the church chest provided the only welfare service—inadequate, always a source of anxiety to Augustine, but at least better than nothing. His sisters had a vital practical part to play.

The growing expectation during the second half of the fourth century that clergy would be unmarried or at least would not cohabit with their wives is illustrated by several texts in Augustine's writings. The motive was mainly ascetic, but was in part connected with the greater authority which, in antiquity, attached to such renunciation.

The novelty of the monastic community as an institutional ingredient in African Catholicism and fear of Augustine's past made many suspicious that he was propagating crypto-Manicheism, an accusation which he was to meet throughout his life in various shapes and forms. During the five or perhaps six years that he served as a priest at Hippo, his main literary efforts were devoted to anti-Manichee polemic. He set out to vindicate first the authority of the book of Genesis, then that of the Church.

Delicate ethical questions were also raised by the Manichees. They complained of the polygamy and vindictive morality of the Israelite patriarchs. In reply Augustine granted that at different times and places what is morally appropriate can vary. Ethical precepts did not need to be as absolute as people often supposed. The Golden Rule (Do not do to others as you would not wish them to do to you) was absolute; its application in different circumstances might produce varying answers. Moreover, what imparts value to an ethical action is the motive with which it is done and the moral consequences of the act. As an external, overt event, an act may be neutral in itself. Sexual intercourse is good and right, indeed a positive duty, in one context; very wrong in another. Yet Augustine allowed that he could envisage very exceptional and rare circumstances in which, with the motive of rescuing her beloved husband from death, a Fidelio-like wife might even go so far as to sleep with his oppressor; and that would be an act of loyalty to her spouse and a means of winning his release. Roman

5

law, public opinion, and the Bible were against men wearing feminine clothing. But no objection would be raised if one used it as a disguise for passing through enemy lines in war, or just because the weather suddenly turned bitterly cold and there was nothing else available. The situation is relevant to judging what is right. Naturally enough, Augustine did not suppose that one could draw up a practical moral code on the basis of the exceptional and unusual.

The distinction between means and ends seemed to him of cardinal importance. Injustice would result as soon as means were treated as ends and vice versa (F 22.78). The distinction was one he could apply to his concept of time and history as a staircase by which we should seek to ascend to the eternal. To seek only goods in time and to neglect eternal good, worse still to treat the eternal good as a tool for obtaining a this-worldly end, is to act unethically. Even one's fellow men may become mere tools for one's self-advancement if they are not respected as deserving to be 'loved in God'. The supreme end of man is to enjoy God for ever. Accordingly Augustine translated the distinction between ends and means into 'enjoyment and use'.

In Augustine's ethics and psychology the will was a central concept and theme. Its operations are indeed hard to account for; but without the will's decision or assent to direct attention to a given matter, one can neither perceive with any understanding, nor acquire scientific knowledge, nor come to faith. The will lies at the heart of an individual's personality. It is directed to whatever is the object of love; and love is like the pull of a weight, dragging the soul wherever it is carried (C xiii.10). Love is both search and delight in its object (S 159.3). The grand moral question to humanity therefore concerns the object(s) of our love, or, in other words, what is supremely important, whether to an individual or to society. Most of Augustine's ethical criticisms of Roman society and government concern either the criminal code's more ferocious enactments or the way in which people spent their money. There the moral values or 'loves' of a society lie naked and open to view.

Plotinus before him had already seen one cause of evil in the perversity of the will rejecting 'interior' (i.e. non-physical) goods and preferring external and inferior goods. For Augustine, man's dilemma is that when he has seen what he ought to do, his will is too weak to do it. The will is indeed in working order for making choices, but the preferred choices are for whatever is comfortable and pleasurable. Hence the problem of the very nature of man, ever restless, ever seeking happiness in places where it cannot be found, knowing not only that he is sick at heart but that he is the very cause of his own sickness (C x.50).

6 Confessions

The old bishop of Hippo who had ordained Augustine presbyter feared lest some other church might carry him off to be their bishop. He therefore persuaded the primate of Numidia to consecrate Augustine to be coadjutor bishop of Hippo. The appointment (irregular in canon law) became surrounded by some controversy. The combination of Augustine's Manichee past and his extreme cleverness helped to make him distrusted. Hippo was not a city where people read books. Numidia was not a province where congregations expected to have a prodigy of intelligence on the episcopal bench. (Augustine noted that illiterate bishops were a favourite butt for the mockery of the half-educated: CR 13). Augustine's presence induced apprehension. He was known to be a terror for demolishing opponents in public disputations. Some did not quite believe in the sincerity of his conversion at Milan.

During his first three years as a bishop Augustine composed his masterpiece, the *Confessions* (a word carrying the double sense of praise and penitence). The work is a prose-poem in thirteen books, in the form of an address to God—a profound modification of the very Neoplatonic *Soliloquies* where Augustine was in dialogue with Reason. In so far as the work had a polemical target, it was directed against the Manichees. There are also dark allusions to stern critics of Augustine's biblical exegesis who stand within the Catholic Church, but are never identified. The schismatic Donatists have not so much as a walk-on part in the play.

He wrote the first nine books in the form of an autobiography down to the time of Monica's death; the ninth book in particular is almost as much about her and his relation to her as about the development of his own mind. The last four books were to describe not the past but the present concerns of his mind as a bishop and expositor of holy scripture. They consist of Neoplatonic analyses of memory, time, creation, and lastly a *tour de force* of subtle exegesis of Genesis 1, interpreted as an allegory about the nature of the Church, the Bible, and the sacraments. The autobiographical sections illustrate a thesis restated in more theological dress by the last four books: the rational creature has turned away from God by neglect, preferring external things and the illusion that happiness consists in bodily satisfaction. Therefore the soul falls below its own level and disintegrates, like the prodigal son reduced to feeding on pigswill. But at the deepest abyss of the ego ('memory' is Augustine's word for everything not at the top of the mind) the soul retains a longing for reintegration and completeness. This is realized in the love of God, and the example and expiation of Christ as the mediator, and proclaimer of that love. God has made us for himself, and the heart is ever unquiet until it finds rest in him.

The *Confessions* narrate Augustine's conversion, and the scene in the Milan garden is told with a rich mosaic of literary echoes. Critical comparison with the Cassiciacum dialogues written soon afterwards shows that in essentials the later retrospect of the *Confessions* gives a reliable story, though clothed in quasi-poetic dress. At first sight there is a contrast between the stormy and passionate *Confessions* and the serene inquiring atmosphere of the Cassiciacum dialogues. Augustine himself first drew attention to the difference of mood, remarking that he found the urbane tone of Cassiciacum too secular and scholastic in spirit. It is nonsense to say that the Cassiciacum texts are more Platonizing than the *Confessions*, where the influence of Plotinus and Porphyry is demonstrably no less ubiquitous. But thirteen years have passed, and Augustine was now responsible for ministering the word and sacraments to his people. The *Confessions* show a profounder engagement with St Paul.

Augustine became persuaded that the inner moral conflict

described in Romans 7 was not just a personified portrait of man not yet under grace, but a self-portrait of Paul with a divided mind uncommonly like his own. Man, noblest of God's earthly creation, gifted with extraordinary intelligence and capacities for social cooperation, has become antisocial by inner corrosion (CD xii.28), by a perversion of the will and by consequent imprisonment in evil habit. In a cosmos of supreme order and beauty humanity and its egotism sound the jarring note. The morbidity of the human heart is illustrated by that split second of shaming secret pleasure when one learns of someone else's misfortune, or by the desire to do something forbidden not because it is enjoyable in itself but merely because it is forbidden—a truth which Augustine underlined with the story of his teenage delinquency in stealing pears, not because he had any taste for them, but because it was a lawless escapade, a re-enactment of the fruit taken by Eve and Adam. He saw his own story as that of Everyman.

At first sight the structure of the *Confessions* is puzzling. After nine books of autobiography culminating in a deeply touching description of his mother's death and requiem, it baffles the uninitiated that he goes on to speak of memory, time, and creation. The last four books actually carry the clue to the whole. Augustine understood his own story as a microcosm of the entire story of the creation, the fall into the abyss of chaos and formlessness, the 'conversion' of the creaturely order to the love of God as it experiences griping pains of homesickness. What the first nine books illustrate in his personal exploration of the experience of the prodigal son is given its cosmic dimension in the concluding parts of the work. The autobiographical sections are related as an accidental exemplification of the wandering homelessness of man's soul in 'the region of dissimilarity' (Plato's phrase for the material realm far removed from the divine). The wanderer is like a dehydrated traveller in a waterless desert, or a lover longing to see the distant beloved (P 37.14). Throughout his life he was peculiarly interested in the study of infant behaviour as a special source of understanding for the student of human nature. In the *Confessions* he set out to show that human beings do not begin their lives in innocence, trailing clouds of glory, which then become darkened by the adult environment. No creature is more selfish, he thought, than the baby in the cot: 'If infants do no injury, it is for lack of strength, not for lack of will' (C i.11). To comprehend the antics of adults negotiating a hard-nosed commercial transaction one need only watch tiny children at play. And then there is the misery of school. The acquisition of mental skills is a toil no less awful than the back-breaking labour to which Adam's fall condemned him. Augustine remarked that the intellectual worker's toil is worse, for at least the manual worker sleeps well.

Friendship is a God-given solace in a tough world (CD xix.8). To Augustine Monica was the supreme friend. He recognized that her love and ambition and possessiveness included a worldly element. Though a citizen of Zion, 'she still lived in the suburbs of Babylon'. But the exalted language of grateful affection towards his mother sometimes passes into the sort of thing he would say of mother Church. A climax of the *Confessions* occurs in book 9 where Augustine described a mystical experience shared by Monica and himself at Ostia when her death was approaching. They spoke together of the transience of all earthly things with their beauty and glory, in contrast with the eternal wisdom of God. For a moment they felt as if their conversation had caught them up into a timeless world. Augustine expressly noted that he was using language in his book which they did not actually use at the time. The passage is rich in phrases drawn from Plotinus, and illustrates how the Neoplatonists provided a language for talking about his experience (C ix.24–5).

Some of the profoundest analyses in the *Confessions* appear in the treatment of memory in the tenth book. The discussion is independent of both Aristotle and Plotinus.

The identity and continuity of the self is seen as rooted in memory/It is a level of the mind which imparts unity to a multiplicity of disconnected experiences in the stream of time. Lying deeper than knowing and willing, memory is 'the stomach of the mind' (C x.21), a storehouse only potentially in the consciousness. Through the universal quest of humanity for happiness, it is also the medium through which the person becomes responsive to grace (C x.29). Augustine did not say that the natural man apart from grace already has God in his subconscious, even when denying or ignoring him with the conscious levels of his personality. To remember God is a conscious act of will, a decision. The love of God is 'no indeterminate feeling, but a certitude of the consciousness' (C x.8).

Yet he did not think God is found by humanity other than in the deepest abyss of the 'memory', present to the mind of the person who wills to order his life in obedience (C x.37). This reflection evokes one of the most famous texts of the Confessions: 'At long last I came to love you, beauty so ancient, yet ever new.' There follows the declaration 'You command continence; give what you command, and command what you will' (below, p. 108).

The tenth book continues with an examination of the extent to which, now a bishop, Augustine had come to self-mastery in face of the attractions bombarding his mind through the five senses. The passage closely resembles an extant text of Porphyry. In the *Confessions* the problem lay not so much in what the senses perceive as in the mind's consenting. 'I have become my own problem' (C x.50). The tenth book ends with a confession of self-surrender to the forgiving grace of God, pledged in the sacrament of the eucharist—a very un-Platonic theme. This leads, however, into an elaborate inquiry into the nature of time.

Time was a major topic on the agenda of Neoplatonic philosophers, partly because of Plato's remarks in the *Timaeus* about eternity, partly because of the paradoxes in the fourth book of Aristotle's *Physics* showing that time is unreal. Aristotle bequeathed a potent awareness of the complexity of the question. Augustine remarked 'I know what time is until somebody asks me' (C xi.17). Plotinus had said much the same, only less trenchantly. Augustine differed from Plotinus in that he did not hold that the self is timeless. The soul is created out of nothing. It is involved from the start in the process of successiveness. But then there is the question whether salvation can be deliverance out of time, a question acute for a Christian theologian who believed that God, himself changeless and transcending both time and place, had acted in time for the redemption of humanity. Augustine was evidently familiar with Aristotle's paradoxes, especially with his argument that the past exists no longer, the future not yet, while the present is an instant without that extension which our notions of time appear to require.

Plato had spoken of past, present, and future as forms of time which seek to imitate the simultaneity of eternity. Most Platonists spoke of time as defined in terms of the movements of the heavenly bodies. Plotinus defined time in psychological terms as the experience of the soul in moving from one state of life to another.

Augustine was of course aware that we ordinarily reckon time by the sun and moon—'a year being 365¼ days, the ¼ requiring an intercalary day to be inserted every four years' (GL ii.29). But in the *Confessions* the analysis of time is set in the context of mysticism as a timeless awareness of the eternal. So he did not want to define time in astronomical terms, nor as the movement of any physical object. Successiveness and multiplicity are simply the experience of the soul in the flux of history. Because multiplicity is a mark of inferiority in a Platonic structure, the transience and mortality of our condition must be in one sense painful. Time presupposes change (C xi.9), and 'change is a kind of death' (Jo 38.10). But in its nature time is a dimension of the mind, a psychological condition attaching to being creaturely. Indeed even the angels, themselves also created, are somehow halfway between time and eternity. But of God we must say that he is unchanging and therefore timeless. He knows past and future, but not as we do in a psychological experience of successiveness. Strictly speaking, therefore, it is a misnomer to speak of divine *fore*knowledge. God knows past and future but not, as we do, in a procession of events.

On this basis Augustine met the questions, Why did God create when he did? Why not sooner? What was he doing before he decided to create? It was a serious matter. Augustine deplored the frivolity of the witty answer that before creation God was preparing hell for curious questioners. The correct reply he thought to be that before creation there can be no time; time and creation are made simultaneously. (To put creation earlier by a finite number of years does nothing to change the question; to say it could have happened an infinite period earlier is to use words with no clear meaning.)

Pagan intellectuals attacked Christianity for supposing that whether in creation or in incarnation, or indeed in answering petitionary prayer, God would be changing his mind, or doing something new. They regarded it as axiomatic that only the everlasting cycle of the cosmic process, into which no particularity can possibly intrude, can be reconciled with the rationality of God. In Augustine's eyes this position locked the world into a finite system. The pagan cosmos had no room for infinity, but only for what is limited and relative. In the twelfth book of the *City of God* Augustine mounted a full-scale assault on the dogma of the eternal cosmic cycle. It had no room for creativity, uniqueness, the absoluteness of divine grace.

On the other hand many sermons of Augustine warned that prayer is neither informing God nor cajoling him into a change of mind, but is the way to conform our wills to his. For God's will and purpose are 'sempiternal'. Not only God but indeed man can will a change without changing his will, without being inconsistent overall with long-term

72

designs. Moreover, Augustine was deeply aware of the
dangers of disappointment in petitionary prayer. In such experiences one ought to reflect that we often love the wrong
things, and that if our prayers were then answered positively it could be a manifestation of divine wrath. Answers to
some egocentric prayers could be punishments (P 26.ii.7).
He knew well enough the hazard of excessive anthropomor-
phism. Of the unchanging presence of God to his world, he
wrote confidently: 'The Creator maintains the created
order from the innermost and supreme hinge-point of
causation' (T iii.16). Among the things the pagan
philosophers did not see he numbered the fact that time and
the historical process have critical turning-points in the
hidden wisdom of God (CD ix.22).

Augustine perceived the problem of God's relation to his
world to turn on the question whether (a) creation issues
from the sole goodness of God by spontaneous outflow, as
an inevitable almost physical emanation, or (b) if the creation results from the omnipotent will of a wholly self-
sufficient First Cause which does not in any sense need the
created order. The former model tends to use physical
analogies like the diffusion of light or the growth of a plant.
The latter model sounds like a glorification of autocratic ar-
bitrariness as a divine characteristic. Is the creation caused
by an overflowing of divine goodness, or by an inexplicable
decision of the divine will? Augustine did everything in his
power to avoid this dilemma of nature or will. He warmed
to a proposition found in Plotinus that in God substance
and will are inseparable.

What then of miracles? Augustine saw order as the
supreme manifestation of providence. But the omnipotent
Creator may surely have an order and design which include
not merely the natural environment but the special case of
his free rational creation. Unusual events can occur as part
of the providential purpose of giving an erring mankind ad-
monition and instruction; that we call a miracle. But the
spiritual Christian does not look for physical miracles.

Augustine

There is no greater miracle than the inner transformation of repentance and faith. For the post-apostolic age the counterpart of New Testament miracles, the swaddling clothes of an infant Church (PM ii.52), should be sought in the sacraments of baptism and eucharist (B iii.21). In old age Augustine came to modify this position. Cures were taking place at the shrines of some African martyrs. Popular devotion prized relics (hawked by charlatans), soil brought from the Holy Land, holy oil from St Stephen's shrine when some bones reached Africa. Nevertheless, the more mature a believer was in the faith, the less he would look for visible wonders (PM ii.52). He did not encourage his flock to seek special providences: the sacraments were enough.

Augustine regarded neither petitionary prayer nor miracle as involving a change in the mind and purpose of God. Requests to God for the necessaries of life, for physical health, for the fertility of one's spouse, he did not think the highest form of prayer; but they did not rank as unworthy petitions, like a prayer for the death of a relative so that one might inherit a legacy. They constituted an acknowledgement that all good things are the gift of the one God, not of inferior pagan deities (P 66.2). But except for sudden moments of arrow-like aspiration, prayer needed silence and solitude (QS ii.4.4). Augustine did not follow Porphyry's argument that petitionary prayer entails the (Aristotelian) conclusion that in God's providence there remain contingent events and coincidences which are not predetermined. On Augustine's assumption God has determined both effects and causes, but the prayers which God hears are among the secondary causes that God uses to bring about his will (O ii.51).

7 Unity and division

The aftermath of the Great Persecution under Diocletian (303) left the African churches divided. They did not agree on the point at which one could or could not compromise with the secular power; African Christians held strongly apocalyptic beliefs. They read the Revelation of St John to mean that Christ would literally return to earth and reign with his saints for a thousand years, a doctrine shared by Augustine himself at first—until he came to interpret the millennium allegorically of heaven. Apocalyptic beliefs commonly went hand in hand with a highly negative view of the imperial government as an agent of virtue, and pessimistic opinions were easily spread among the agrarian small-holders and tenant farmers of Numidia. The edicts of the pagan emperor forbidding Christians to meet for worship and requiring the surrender of sacred books and vessels moved enthusiastic Christians to study the heroic story of the Maccabees and their fierce resistance to Antiochus Epiphanes more than four centuries earlier. But there was a sharp division of ethical judgement between the hawks and the doves. Christian hawks absolutely refused to co-operate with the secular authorities. The doves wanted no confrontations, but only to live quiet lives of modest virtue. Among the doves were the bishop of Carthage and his archdeacon, who regarded the zealots as provocative and undeserving of the title of martyr or 'confessor' (the early Christian term for one who confessed the faith before the governor and suffered torture and imprisonment, but was not granted the supreme gift of martyrdom). Even before the persecution broke out, there was deep disagreement among the Christians of Africa about whether it was right for acts of vandalism to be committed against pagan shrines as citadels of demonic corruption, or whether such acts merely generated hatred of the Church among pagan worshippers, and failed to respect the sincerity of the pagan intention.

In 311 the bishop of Carthage died and the doves' party acted fast. They hastily gathered three bishops to lay hands on the archdeacon as his successor. It was widely believed that the principal consecrator was one of those bishops who eight years before had surrendered sacred books or vessels to the confiscating authorities. The hawks brought in the old primate of Numidia with a very large body of supporting bishops, and a rival bishop was consecrated. After some uneasy negotiations, the Numidian candidate was recognized neither by the churches north of the Mediterranean nor by the emperor Constantine the Great. From thenceforth until the Muslim invasion of Africa two rival groups existed, each with its own episcopate, each reciting the same creed, each with identical sacramental forms and liturgical structures. Altar was erected against altar in every city and village.

The Numidian faction came to be led by Donatus, their bishop in Carthage. The Donatists rejected the Catholic community, which in Numidia was a minority group both in town and countryside, and despised it as the puppet of the secular government, an instrument of political ends, polluted by a consistent record of compromise with worldliness. Donatists refused to acknowledge the validity and purity of Catholic sacraments of any kind, so that in their eyes Augustine was a schismatic and heretical layman. Group distrust and rancour became inveterate. Both sides discouraged mixed marriages and made canonical enactments against them. It was very common for families to be divided. Augustine himself had a Donatist cousin.

The Donatists held with deep passion that they alone were safeguarding the authentic holiness and ritual purity of God's temple, the Church. To defend their refusal to recognize sacraments given outside the pure Church they could appeal, with reason, to the writings of Roman Africa's greatest Christian hero, St Cyprian bishop of Carthage, martyred in 258. The claims of the Catholic Church to be the one true communion seemed to the Donatists utterly invalidated by their toleration of the catastrophic sin of apostasy. The Catholic bishop of Carthage, and indeed the bishop of Rome himself if he supported the African Catholics (as indeed he did), were agents of Antichrist sitting where he ought not in the very sanctuary of God. Some Donatists even said that, instead of being some sort of holy communion service, a Catholic mass was a corrupt ceremony at which nameless blasphemy was enacted. Donatist tradesmen would not deal with Catholic clergy if they could avoid it.

To the critical contention that God could hardly have intended his universal Church to be reduced to one small region of the empire, the Donatists replied that particularity was the very principle of the incarnation; that on moral issues minorities are generally right, the silent majority being another name for spineless compromisers; and above all that the holiness of the Church is prior to and the ground of its unity and unicity. Both Donatist and Catholic agreed that Noah's Ark prefigured redemption through the one Church of Christ. It gave the Donatists satisfaction to think the Ark contained only eight persons.

When Augustine became a bishop, he found the two communities numbly resigned to eighty-five years of mutual hostility and absolute distrust. The rancour was well sustained on the Donatist side by acts of fearful violence against Catholic buildings and clergy. The zealots who had once assaulted pagan shrines now found a new target in Catholic basilicas, where they would smash the wooden altar over the head of the poor Catholic bishop if he were so unwise as to be available. The list of Catholic clergy who suffered maiming, or blinding when lime and vinegar were thrown into their eyes, or outright death, was not short. Augustine himself once escaped a Donatist ambush intended to silence him for ever, only because his guide mistook the road. Donatist bishops publicly deplored the violence, which was mainly organized by the rural clergy.

Augustine saw that it was essential to provide the Catholic community with an effective arsenal of the theological argument. He moved the Catholic bishops to hold a series of synods at which they could form a united front and common policy. The primate of Carthage, a humble man who much depended on Augustine to write his sermons for him, was very ready to give a lead if Augustine would advise him what to do. Augustine argued from biblical prophecies about the extension of God's rule over all the earth, not merely in Africa. Moreover, the parables of the kingdom (Matt. 13) taught that in the Lord's field both wheat and tares should be left until the harvest of the last judgement. Therefore no scandal could ever be sufficient ground to introduce division and to leave the one Church. Noah's Ark was a sign that it is indispensable to stay in the Church if one is not to perish in the Flood. For Augustine the eight persons in the Ark symbolized the Church's inner core of spiritually minded faithful, who had to endure the stink of less rational company but much preferred that to drowning. As for the Donatist claim that the rest of the Christian world had become guilty of apostasy by association, 'the whole world judges that without the least anxiety': *securus judicat orbis terrarum* (EP iii.24). Indeed 'it is a characteristic mark of all heretics that they are unable to see what is perfectly obvious to everyone else' (ii.5).

Among the marks of a true believer Augustine specified that he would always love the Church, warts and all. He did not deny that at the time of the Great Persecution some bishops had improperly compromised with the government. He too admired the Maccabees and their fervent zeal for God. But the errors of individual bishops could not bring pollution on a community or upon an episcopal succession. The grace of God did not depend for its efficacy on the personal sanctity of the individual minister, but on whether he did what God commanded to be done and thereby showed himself aware that in his sacramental action the whole Church is acting. For every act of the Church is catholic, universal. The sacrament is Christ's, not the minister's personal property, and salvation is always and throughout the work of God, not of man. Therefore a sacrament of baptism bestowed by an orthodox but schismatic priest must on no account be repeated. Baptism has stamped the soul with a decisive once-for-all seal, just as Christ died once-for-all to redeem. Admittedly, baptism given in schism could not be fully a means of grace until the recipient had been reconciled to the Church. On the same principles, Augustine flatly denied that, even when a line of ordinations stemmed from a bishop guilty of mortal sin, there could be transmission of defilement.

Donatist atrocities by the zealots of Numidia finally moved the imperial government to adopt a stronger policy of state coercion against the schismatics. Initially Augustine had the strongest reservations about the deployment of force by the government, and his doubts were shared by many Catholic bishops in Africa. He did not deny that coercion to restrain acts of criminal violence was legitimate, but to put pressure on the Donatists to join the Catholic Church under threat of fines or of being deprived of the right to bequeath property seemed to Augustine highly inexpedient. It would produce either hypocritical conversions or a great increase in unstoppable acts of terror, or even Donatist suicides. Under strong government pressure, the Numidian zealots used to throw themselves over cliffs, and their deaths hugely increased the odium with which Donatists regarded the Catholic community who were held responsible.

Augustine hated violence. He sternly rebuked fellow-Catholics who spoke uncharitably of the Donatists (E 61.1; 65.5). Argument did not comfortably lie with coercion. Augustine's theology included the doctrine, surprising to many of his contemporaries, that all Donatist sacraments, including ordination, were valid. He saw that this would remove a major barrier to corporate reunion and perhaps, simultaneously, solve a problem for the Catholic community which was extremely short of clergy to staff its parishes. Moreover, the Donatists included many Christians of honest and good heart, among whom he felt sure that God numbered some of his elect. They would show themselves to be truly elect if they came to adhere to God's true Church.

In practice, the government policy of coercion had astonishing success, especially among property owners and traders in the towns, less so at first among the Punic-speaking peasants of the countryside; but many of them also came over in time, and Augustine then had the difficult task of finding fluent Punic speakers for rural bishoprics. Many lay people in Africa frankly regarded it as a matter of ultimate indifference for salvation which communion one belonged to. Among the peasants there were rice-Christians ready to go along with whichever faction better cared for their material interests. The misery and torment of the schism made many revert to their old paganism. In Numidia intimidation played a substantial part in main-taining Donatist loyalty, and converts from Donatism to Catholicism were peculiarly liable to be mugged.

The process of reconciliation occupied a very large pro-portion of Augustine's time and energy over a great number of years. Reunion was accelerated after a large conference at Carthage in 411 where Donatist and Catholic bishops con-fronted one another under the presiding hand of a (Catholic) imperial commissioner entrusted with giving a verdict be-tween the contending parties. Augustine was principal spokesman for the Catholic cause. He persuaded the Catholic bishops to begin by publicly declaring that if the Donatists would take communion with them and unite, they would then invite their Donatist opposite numbers to share in the pastorate of each diocese. The generous offer cost nothing. The mutual rancour was too great for the pro-posal to have any chance of acceptance.

The government's intention in summoning the conference, with a predetermined verdict in favour of the Catholics, was to justify a subsequent policy of steady pressure on the Donatist laity. Could coercion be justified on any grounds other than practical success? Unfortunately Augustine saw how much good the government pressure was doing. In his own city of Hippo a Catholic minority was converted into a majority. He decided to offer a theoretical defence which would meet the anxieties of Catholic bishops who felt that no force or social pressure should be used to unite anyone to the Church, and that the Church had enough hypocrites of its own already without welcoming to its bosom a large body of alienated and explicitly insincere adherents. Augustine soon discovered that among the Donatist converts there were many devout and virtuous people he was glad to have. The process of conversion was in any event a lifelong affair, never a matter of a sudden flash. Even the sullen and alienated would surely come to see in time that the pressure to reunite with the Church was for their own good, since it was for their salvation now and hereafter. The lord in the gospel parable of the wedding feast told his servants to fill his table by compelling people to come in. A greater Lord ejected traders from the Temple with a scourge of small cords. To spare chastisement is not always the act of wise and loving parents. A surgeon cannot cure without causing pain, but his purpose is remedial.

Select quotations from Augustine's anti-Donatist writings enabled some medieval canonists to make him look as if he were justifying the stern measures against heretics adopted in the later middle ages. Augustine would have been horrified by the burning of heretics, by the belief, found not only among sixteenth-century Protestants and medieval Catholics but even in the medieval world of Byzantine Orthodoxy, that heretical ideas are of so insidious and diabolical a nature that the only available way of stopping them is to exterminate the propagators. In late medieval times people came to think of heretics in the way

81

some today regard murdering hijackers or pushers of hard drugs, in practice difficult to eliminate without killing. They appealed to texts picked out of Augustine's works to justify severity, and ignored the numerous places where he wholly opposed torture and capital punishment or any discipline that went beyond what a truly loving father might administer to an erring son. Especially after the revocation of the edict of Nantes in France, the apologists for the repression of the Huguenots looked to Augustine for help. When he wrote 'Love and do as you like' (EJo 7.8 and elsewhere), the context shows that he regarded this epigrammatic formula as providing both a justification for the discipline of the erring and also a principle of great restraint in the manner of that discipline.

The Donatists protested that the actions of the imperial government against them did not feel like love; that it was in principle wrong for the Catholic Church to make use of force provided by the secular arm; that a body which resorted to persecution *ipso facto* discredited itself from ability to represent the word of Christ. Augustine did not think such protests entirely plausible in the mouths of a party responsible for an immense catalogue of violent acts against Catholics in Africa. Nor did he think 'paternal rebuke' of criminal dissidence amounted to persecution.

To Augustine it finally seemed axiomatic that action bringing one into the authentic fold, even if a little uncomfortable, is love. But of course the means used to achieve that end had to be carefully watched, and should not go beyond the imposition of mild disabilities on property owners or, in the case of rustic labourers, a moderate flogging.

One major difference between Augustine and the Donatists lay in the doctrine of the perfection of the Church militant here in earth. Donatists quoted St Paul's saying that the Church is 'without spot or blemish'. They granted that, even among their own number, there were individuals who received the sacraments and then turned out to remain as unreconstructed as before. But the failures of individuals, clergy and laity, were not at all the same thing as the pollution of the Church. This they affirmed to be the very body of Christ, the locus of holiness, the society of saints, guaranteed by the unquestioned apostolic succession of their bishops.

Apostolic succession mattered to the African Catholics too, for it was the external form that helped to safeguard the sacred tradition of apostolic teaching and sacraments. But it was not stressed except when they were speaking of the succession to St Peter in the Roman see with which they enjoyed communion while the Donatists (since 313) did not. Augustine thought that the Donatists could not plausibly claim to be the one true Catholic Church when they were in communion with 'neither Rome nor Jerusalem'. He did not think Peter personally was the rock on which the Church was built, though at the end of his life he noted that some interpreters took the text in St Matthew that way, and allowed that it was very possible. Normally he understood the 'rock' to be Peter's confession of faith in Christ the Son of God; and 'we Christians believe not in Peter but in him in whom Peter believed' (CD 18.54). Peter is frequently presented by him as a symbol of the universality and unity of the one Church. When he speaks of 'apostolic sees' he often uses the plural (DDC ii.12).

However, like all other African bishops of the Catholic community, Augustine was very conscious of the fact that the Catholic *raison d'être* in largely Donatist provinces like Numidia depended on communion with Rome. He took it for granted that the Roman see could exercise a dispensing power if the rigorous operation of conciliar canon law was producing great awkwardness. He assumed that on African church affairs the African bishops could give an independent synodical judgement; but they were glad when Roman authority reinforced their verdict. Where that had happened, it was surely the end of the matter under debate—*causa finita est* (S 131 and elsewhere). On the other hand, the

African bishops cordially hated it when clergy disciplined in Africa appealed directly to the Roman see, and when the Popes did not fully inform themselves about the cases in question. In the year 418 there was a notorious instance of a delinquent presbyter named Apiarius, suspended by his bishop; he appealed to the Pope (Zosimus) and received so benevolent a hearing that the African bishops were much offended by the slight to their autonomy and asked pertinent questions about the canon law under which the Pope alleged his authority to decide. Finally they themselves enacted a formal canon 'that none may dare to appeal to the Roman Church'.

Augustine much regretted the Pope's imprudence over Apiarius, and the same Pope's willingness to listen to other heretics, but significantly did his best to whitewash these affairs. He felt sure that no bishop of Rome would make the mistake of reaching a verdict contrary to the general mind of the episcopate.

Of the Church as the body of Christ Augustine used lyrical language. The word and sacraments entrusted to the Church were the very means and instruments of salvation. So the Church is the Dove or the beloved Bride of the Song of Songs; the society of all faithful people; the body of which Christ is so inseparably head that 'the whole Christ' is the Lord and his Church indissolubly together; the body of which the Holy Spirit is the soul. The Church militant and the Church triumphant were symbolized by Martha and Mary (Luke 10), symbols of the active and the contemplative. But in this life the empirical Catholic community is not without spot. Individual lapses and mistakes are many and great.

Augustine did not share the pessimistic view of his friend Jerome that the contemporary Church was prefigured by the Israel of the Old Testament, denounced by the prophets as having a unique propensity to apostasy. His portrait of the clergy of his time shows that both quantity and quality were low, and that scandals were not infrequent. He knew that among the laity some of the baptized fell into mortal sins, and then had to be told that they could not come to the eucharist until absolved. But mortal sins were grave matters such as flagrant adultery or theft. Venial sins were to be cleansed by daily use of the Lord's Prayer and by almsgiving.

Donatist language about the ordained ministry as the supreme guarantee of their sacraments seemed to Augustine to presuppose a much too clericalized notion of the Church. The ministry had a very necessary service to perform. Ordination was a sanctification by the Holy Spirit. It was self-evident that the presidency at the eucharist should be given to those commissioned by ordination for this work. No one (except in heretical sects) dreamt of lay presidency. But Augustine never thought of the Church as consisting in the clergy. The ministry was subordinate, a service. The continuity of the Church in the apostolic faith had its instrument and sign in ministerial order, but when in his refutation of Mani's so-called *Fundamental Letter*, Augustine looked for authentication of the truth of the gospel he looked to the faith of the universal church: 'I would not have believed the gospel if the authority of the universal Church had not constrained me to do so.' The converse of this sentence is not one that he would have denied.

Augustine did not think that God spoke to man exclusively through appointed means of grace, through Bible and sacraments, but these were certainly the central and normal media. In themselves both the human words of scripture and the water, bread, and wine of baptism and eucharist are frail earthly elements. But God makes them his own instruments, and to the believing heart they convey truth and grace. Without faith the sacraments do not profit the soul. Therefore 'believe and you have eaten' (Jo 25.12). Sacraments are signs; but 'scripture speaks of signs as being the reality signified' (Jo 63.2). Augustine's eucharistic language employs both the symbolist language congenial to a Platonist, inclined to be embarrassed by the externality of the sacramental sign, and the realist language characteristic of the Bible and closely linked with the eschatological theme of the actualization of the kingdom of God here and now. So we find a distinction drawn between the sacrament and the *res* or reality (Augustine did not mean anything material) which is conveyed thereby (Jo 26.15; CD x.20; xxi.25.4). Controversy with the Donatists led him to lay emphasis on the interior reception by the soul, while controversy with the Manichees prevented him from supposing that the elements of the eucharist are too earthy to be used by God.

8 Creation and the Trinity

About the time Augustine completed the *Confessions*, his mind was already turning towards two topics which, in the intervals of Donatist affairs, occupied his few leisure moments for the next fifteen and more years. These topics were, first, the exegesis of the first three chapters of Genesis, and, secondly, the doctrine of the Trinity. Both were areas in which pagan intellectuals were much inclined to mock. As an account of God creating the world, Genesis 1 seemed to suggest creation was all at once and instantaneous. Philosophers (or at least some of them) thought of it as a process in which the divine Artist did the best he could with formless matter. The story of Adam and Eve and the Serpent seemed a naïve myth. Most Platonists admitted the language of 'creation' in speaking of God's relation to the cosmos; Plato had used the word in the *Timaeus*. But they thought this figurative language for a timeless dependence; in reality the cosmos was eternal, and had neither beginning nor end.

Augustine composed five expositions of Genesis, including *Confessions* 11–12 and *City of God* 11. His first was an allegorical commentary in refutation of Manichee criticism. But allegory was vulnerable to the charge of being a sophistical device to avoid embarrassing difficulties. Augustine began a literal commentary, but that was never completed. About 401 he began a massive commentary on the literal sense of the book, which ranks as one of his major achievements. The twelve books of his *Exposition of the Literal Meaning of Genesis* begin from the assumption that, if he was not here treating Genesis 1–3 as an allegory about the Church and sacraments, sin and grace, nor could he regard the opening of Genesis as a piece of 'Creation Science'. It was awkward when Christians talked as if the

Bible offered an alternative explanation of the world in rivalry to that of astronomers and other natural scientists. It made them and their faith look foolish, and obscured the really important matters which Christians had to say.

Galileo warmly approved of Augustine's remarks on this subject. Augustine's commentary betrays a strong interest in questions we would classify as scientific, but at the same time refuses to impose a decision in obscure matters merely on the ground that the sacred text was being taken by some as a handbook of natural science.

'Literal' in Augustine's understanding did not mean that the sacred author was giving a matter-of-fact account. Nevertheless Genesis did mean the world was actually created. Both the existence of humanity and that of the cosmos are dependent on the will and goodness of God. In this sense of the term 'literal', Augustine understood Genesis to be telling us what is the case, and not to be a complicated way of talking about the eternity of the world and an inherent immortality of the soul. He did not suppose that to speak of God's existence as First Cause is a way of saying that the universe came to be at the start of a finite period of time. Whereas most Platonists thought the creator should be understood on the analogy of an artist or craftsman doing his best with the recalcitrant sludge of matter, since the second century Christian theologians had been assertive that the creator also made matter, and the world is 'out of nothing'. Porphyry's commentary on the *Timaeus* of Plato helped Augustine here; Porphyry had there said that while matter is in the order of being prior to the form the Creator has given it, nevertheless there was never a moment in time when it lacked form. Augustine made this language his own, and (as Porphyry himself observed) it met the strictest demands of monotheism.

The notion of an instantaneous act of creation suggested to the philosophers a kind of conjuring trick. Augustine saw that the world was a developing process. Not everything in the world now was created so in the beginning. God, he thought, had created 'seminal principles' or causal reasons for everything that subsequently came to be, and this language allowed him to envisage new genera appearing later. Neoplatonic language about the evolutionary development of the grades in the hierarchy of being may have provided him here with a vocabulary. Plotinus' language about 'emanation' may also have influenced him. It was a Neoplatonic axiom that all effects are contained in potentiality in their causes. He did not think chance or randomness played a part in the amazing order and design of the world. 'Chance' is a term used when we do not happen to know the cause (Ac. i.1). Nothing occurs without a cause of some sort (CD v.9). Augustine was confident of the rationality of the universe; only the quirks of free choices introduced apparent irrationalities.

Augustine has a reputation for disparaging the feminine sex. This can be supported by selective quotation; but some utterances are very positive. He opposed the current exposition of St Paul's words (1 Cor. 11:7) according to which the male, not the female, is made in God's image. He held that men and women are differentiated in body, not in soul or powers of mind. On the other hand, he took it to be self-evident that the prime function of woman is biological. 'Had Adam needed a helpmeet in the sense of a partner in really intelligent conversation and companionship, God would surely have provided another man; in providing Eve his intention was to ensure the continuance of the race' (GL ix.9). He assumed that in marriage the wife's role is to be domestic and supportive, like Monica tolerating and tranquillizing even a hot-tempered and none too faithful partner. The partners were to 'walk side by side' (BC i.1)—perhaps regretting the custom, still common in parts of the world today, by which the husband walked in front with the wife carrying babies and baggage behind. Unequal in public life, husband and wife were absolutely equal in conjugal rights (F 22.31; QH iv.59).

A number of Augustine's sayings illustrate the

commonplace that generalized attitudes to women are often determined by attitudes to sexuality. The man who had once adhered to the ascetic Manichees and simultaneously lived with a woman to meet his erotic need could be expected to be inconsistent. His conversion to Catholic Christianity enforced a positive evaluation of the body which was potentially at odds with the fact that renunciation of sex lay at the nerve-centre of his decision. One sermon proclaims the lawfulness of delight in the wonders of nature, music, flowers and scents, good food, 'and conjugal embraces' (S 159.2). In the *City of God* (xxii.17) he vehemently rejects the notion of some that in the world to come the resurrection will bring both men and women into male bodies, as if femininity had been a regrettable error by the Creator. On the other hand, he feared sexuality (not least in himself) as passing easily out of rational control. Even the sisters in the Hippo nunnery were warned that a woman can unconsciously and unintentionally throw a man off balance merely by a flashing eye (E 211).

The *Literal Exposition of Genesis* is not pervaded by polemical passages, but offers many discussions of problems concerning the idea of creation and the nature of man. The tension between Platonism and the Bible is apparent throughout, and it is possible to read the commentary as marking a stronger awareness that he had to put more distance between the two than he had once thought in his Cassiciacum days. Porphyry, not mentioned by name in the text, was a major figure in the background of the commentary. Because the book has relatively little polemic, its character is markedly exploratory and tentative. When in the *Revisions* of his old age Augustine looked back on the work, he felt that it was all too conjectural and provisional to be a useful book. The modern reader is most unlikely to agree with this adverse verdict.

An engagement with Neoplatonism appears even more strikingly in many parts of the fifteen books *On the Trinity*, a work he finally completed when he was sixty-five. The first seven books examine the tradition of the Church, first in scripture, then in the orthodox commentators and theologians. The masterful work written a generation earlier by Hilary of Poitiers on the same subject greatly impressed him. One of the central questions addressed by both Hilary and Augustine was one especially associated with Arius, an Alexandrian parish priest early in the fourth century. Arius had precipitated a major controversy by his thesis that the doctrine of the divine Triad could be reconciled with monotheism by conceding, or indeed insisting on, the metaphysical and moral subordination of the Son to the Father. Augustine felt, with some reason, that the anti-Arian arguments of orthodox writers, including even the best Greek theologians of the fourth century, had been less effective and forceful than they should have been. They had made too many concessions of principle to Arius' way of thinking. The last eight books explore the possibility of understanding 'three in one' by a series of analogies drawn from human psychology. The two halves of the work therefore corresponded to his antithesis between faith and understanding.

The orthodox tradition rejected not only Arius but also the rival notion, associated with an obscure third-century heretic named Sabellius, that Father, Son, and Spirit are adjectival terms expressing attributes of the one God. In short, it rejected the idea that Father, Son, and Spirit are either merely adjectives or full substantives. To philosophical inquirers among thoughtful non-Christians of the age, this made it look as if the doctrine of the Trinity defied rational understanding. Granted that 'God' is a sublime mystery, yet this way of talking seemed like an unintelligible formula, almost a liturgical incantation impervious to reason. When the subject was mentioned, pagan intellectuals laughed.

Augustine showed effortlessly that the concept of being both one and three is so far from being gobbledygook that simple reflection on the nature of human personality offers

an immediate example. Introspection shows a triad of being, knowing, and willing. These three operations are
mutually interconnected and of equal significance. Similarly there are other triads, such as memory, intelligence, will;
or mind, knowledge, and love; or the lover, the beloved,
and the love that binds them. None of these, however, offered for Augustine a simple ladder up to God, whose image
in man is found not in body but in the mind, in freedom,
reason, and self-consciousness. The analogies crushingly
answered the critics who thought 'three in one' ludicrous
nonsense. But their flexibility and multiplicity of meaning
are too great to enable our minds to make a transfer of these
concepts to God. The nearest and best analogy is reached in
the fifteenth and last book, in the intimate unity of thinking, speaking, and willing, and in the affinity between
knowing and loving.

'Analogy' was a term which, for Augustine and his contemporaries, did not mean a vague resemblance, but rather
something exact and mathematical. In one place he uttered
warnings that for talk about God analogy could be too
precise, and end in being anthropomorphic (S 52). The unity of the mind and its operations he took for granted. He did
not speak of the mind possessing independent faculties or
non-communicating departments. Nevertheless, under the
pressure of his search for 'vestiges' or 'footprints' of the Holy Trinity in the soul of man, his language could sometimes
be taken to suggest quasi-independent parts of the psyche.
The fact betrayed his theological difficulty. He could find
no terms to explain clearly the distinction between Father,
Son, and Holy Spirit. In their works in relation to the world
they are undivided. Since Tertullian at the end of the second century Latin theology had spoken of 'three *personae*
in one substance' (this last term carried no necessarily
material connotation). 'Persona' had come into use because
Tertullian found in the Old Testament, e.g. Psalm 2,
passages which he expounded as dialogue between *dramatis
personae*.

'Substance' was a word which Augustine thought acceptable with qualifications as a term for transcendent
metaphysical Being, as long as it had no implication that in
God there are both substance and accidents. But 'three persons' disturbed him greatly. God transcends all number,
and cannot be counted. Perhaps one could say 'three'
without answering the question 'three what?' 'Three persons' had long been hallowed community tradition in the
Church, and Augustine was respectful of usage in both
philosophy and theology.

Using Aristotelian language Augustine saw the terms
Father and Son to be words expressing relation. So he pro-
posed: The Trinity is one of relations, but not of
substances. The Father is the fount or principle of Godhead,
the Son 'begotten' (i.e. his relation to the Father is internal
to the divine unity and has no analogy to the dependence of
the contingent created order). The Holy Spirit 'proceeds'—
the word came from St John's Gospel.

Latin theology of the generation before Augustine (Hilary
of Poitiers and Ambrose of Milan) had already spoken of the
Holy Spirit as proceeding from the Father and the Son. A
Greek creed accepted at the Council of Constantinople
(381) had said 'proceeding from the Father'; that Council
had no western representation, and made canonical decisions uncongenial to the West. That it had sanctioned a
creed was unknown to the West until more than twenty
years after Augustine's death. There was therefore no
reason why Augustine should hesitate to affirm that the
Spirit proceeds from the Father *and the Son*. He felt that
this way of speaking protected the Trinity from being
understood as an unequal graded Triad; it gave altogether
more emphasis to the unity of God than the Greek formula
did. Very gradually Augustine's formula entered the
liturgical creed in the West. Four centuries later this point
became an issue widening the gap between the Greek East
and Western Christendom. The medieval West defended
the insertion of 'and the Son' (*Filioque*) into the Creed as

resting on papal authority. Even in the sixteenth century the Western Christians who were taken out of communion with Rome kept the Augustinian formula against the original conciliar text. Catholic monasteries in South Italy, on the other hand, did not make the Augustinian addition.

Augustine's work on the Trinity had profound influence on subsequent western concepts of personality. Porphyry had thought that all souls had a share in the 'world-soul', source of all energy and vitality in the physical universe. The early Augustine used the notion of a world-soul. The late Augustine never said there was no such entity, but thought the young Augustine rash to assume that there was: 'For us God is not this world, whether or not there is a world-soul. If there is, God created it. If not, the world cannot be anyone's god, *a fortiori* not ours. But even if there is not a world-soul there is a life-force obeying God working through the angels.' (R i.11.3).

Making the world a god was not the only problem. Porphyry's language tended to locate individuation not in souls but in physical differentiation. To Augustine each soul is distinct, with his or her own personal destiny in the purpose of God. Moreover, the biblical concept of God he saw to stand apart from the Platonic tradition because of the stress on will, on what is creative, original, unique. So the term personality came to mean not only the non-material, interior character of a human being, but also what is distinctive and unshared. Boethius' classical definition of person as 'the individual substance of the rational being' spelt out in detail what was already implicit in Augustine.

The concept of a supreme Triad at the apex of the hierarchy of being was not a notion which could long be mocked by Neoplatonist minds without falling into hopeless inconsistency. Plotinus and Porphyry had worked with such a scheme, with their metaphysic of the One, Mind, and the World-Soul. This helps to explain why in *True Religion* Augustine regarded the doctrine that God is Trinity as being a truth readily accessible to philosophic reason, whereas the incarnation could be apprehended only in the humility of faith. The point reflects Augustine's tenacious hold on the Christian presupposition that the untidy flux of history is the stage of divine self-disclosure: God's saving word to man was embodied, at its nodal and focal point, in a personal historical life, and is witnessed through and in a historical visible community. Platonist though Augustine was, he did not think salvation lay in timeless abstractions. He needed therefore a view of history arising out of and expressing his central religious conviction, an interpretation which would simultaneously offer a vindication of faith in providence despite all the catastrophes of historical experience, and despite the impossibility of adopting anything but a sombre estimate of the present condition of human nature.

History he regarded as the object of a this-worldly knowledge (*scientia*) quite distinct from higher wisdom (*sapientia*). But the Platonic disjunction of the two worlds of sense and mind could be overcome by applying the Christian concept of history as being like a sacramental ladder which God can use, elevating the soul from the active life to the contemplative, from temporal to eternal, through the Jesus of history who becomes the Christ of faith (F 12.26; T 13.24). We are to pass by him on the path to the vision of unchanging eternity (S 88).

9   City of God

The conflict of argument between ancient pagan intellectuals and Christianity is as early as the first century (see Acts 17). The pagan Celsus' attack in the second century was answered by Origen in the third. Porphyry in turn attacked Origen. From Constantine onwards the emperors other than the excitable, shortlived Julian, professed Christianity. But most of the aristocrats and rich landowners, with the peasants on their estates, remained conservative, attached to polytheistic cult. Not that the intellectuals believed the old myths. The gods adored in the temples had long been mocked in the theatres and more politely demolished in lecture-rooms. But the rites were received ways of keeping unseen powers propitious. Neglect surely produced famine, drought, plague, military defeat. To abandon them was to assume one had reason to follow a superior way. On the question of temple cult Neoplatonists were divided. To many what most mattered was the inward purification of the soul; sacrifices, images, and external ceremonies of any kind were a distraction, at best symbols. To others the old rites were important, and became the more so as the Christians attacked them. Fourth-century Neoplatonists could be much given to an obsessive ritualism, in some cases with miraculous phenomena to vindicate their beliefs. They acted in a way that seemed to confirm the Christian identification of pagan cult with sorcery and the occult.

On the question of cult (as we saw earlier) Porphyry wrote with two voices. On the one hand he conceded that the old rites had the weight of immemorial tradition behind them, and no doubt propitiated malevolent spirits. On the other hand, he abhorred animal sacrifices.

About the time Augustine was ordained, imperial policy

set in train a series of edicts closing temples and forbidding pagan sacrifices. The effect was to engender sullen hatred of the Church. More than one anti-Christian riot occurred with substantial loss to life and property. At Rome in 410 pagan aristocrats held special sacrifices to avert Alaric's Goths, while the Christian clergy were begging the intercessions of Peter, Paul, Laurence, and other patron saints of the city. Alaric sacked the city, but his soldiers showed respect for Christian basilicas. Christians thought the catastrophe caused by the existence of too many pagans. The pagans blamed Christian neglect of the old gods, and asked why in Christian times disasters were more numerous. The fall of the eternal city on 24 August 410, which was of greater symbolic than political importance, provoked a discussion of divine providence in history, and debate whether Christianity was about to bring about the collapse of the Roman empire. Against this ferment of argument Augustine began to write 'a large and arduous work', *magnum opus et arduum*, the *City of God*, developing themes which had already appeared in *True Religion* which he wrote as a layman, but now set in an altogether grander perspective.

The title came from the Psalter, and was chosen to offer a conscious contrast to the *Republics* of Plato and Cicero, with whom parts of the work were a running combat. The writing of the twenty-two books of this work occupied thirteen years. He began at the age of fifty-nine and completed it when he was seventy-two.

The first five books replied to polytheists who saw the old gods as uniquely protecting Roman interests. But were not the gods merely deified men? Augustine made much use of an archaic study of Roman religion by the famous scholar Varro, replete with exhausting erudition on the most trivial aspects of pagan cult. One wonders why Augustine compiled his description of polytheism from a book written five centuries previously instead of describing what was going on in Africa until only a few years previously. The contemporary pagan intellectuals, perhaps in self-defence, developed strongly antiquarian interests, as one can see in Macrobius' *Commentary on Scipio's Dream* or his *Saturnalia*. Their argument against Christianity said that it was not the pristine tradition. Augustine set out to show, from unimpeachable authority, just how uninspiring and embarrassing the pristine stuff was.

Books 6–10 were directed to Neoplatonic minds who were reinterpreting the polytheistic tradition as a path of purification, the gods being mediators between humanity and the highest realms. The Platonic writings of his fellow-African Apuleius offered many texts for debate.

Augustine was aware that his friendly but critical discussion of Platonism would shock the contemporary enthusiasts who treated Plato as a sacred authority in whose writings nothing should ever be modified. But in Porphyry he found a modernist reinterpreting the Platonic tradition in radical ways, and thereby bringing it remarkably close to the Christianity Porphyry hated.

Augustine rejected Roman imperialism, Stoic self-sufficiency and (for all his deep admiration and personal debt) Neoplatonic self-purgation as a variety of expressions of pride. The ultimate tension for humanity he saw as being not that between passion and reason, both of which can be equally vehicles of self-assertion. In the fourteenth book of the *City of God* he defended the emotions as good constituents of human nature by the creator's intention, and attacked the Stoic notion that emotion must be suppressed. Loving was a basic human drive; it should be rightly directed, that is to God and our neighbour. The old humanist ideal was to elevate human dignity to equality with the divine. It was to achieve that end that Porphyry's book *On the Return of the Soul* recommended flight from everything bodily. Augustine refused to identify the body with the root of evil. On the other hand he thought it illusion to suppose that man's highest good is attainable in this life and may be found in his magnificent social or

cultural or technological achievements. Man's highest good
lies in eternal life in and with God. This does not entail a
rejection of this life's values; but it does make them
relative.

Some passages in the *City of God* give the impression of
wholly discarding the Roman Empire and all political
institutions as power-hungry organizations for wicked
domination and oppression by the powerful. Sallust's
austere pages on the internecine struggles of Roman
republican history certainly influenced Augustine, and he
quotes with assent Sallust's mordant dictum that Roman
society was characterized by private affluence and public
squalor. Cicero (a casualty of those internecine struggles)
saw that any coherent society must have a system of law,
and would be held together by bonds of mutual interest and
interdependence. Yet Roman history had never ceased to be
a catalogue of aggressive conquests. How could a
polytheistic society be one in which justice could prevail?
'Take away justice, and what are governments but
brigandage on a grand scale?' (CD 4.4).

But now Christian times had come. Could justice now be
established by an emperor acknowledging the true worship
of the one God manifested in Christ? The young Augustine
from time to time wrote as if the answer to that question
was or could be Yes—as if conversion to Christianity was
bringing regeneration to a tired and sick society and was
making possible 'a just empire' (E 138.14); as if by imperial
legislation supporting the Catholic Church against pagan
cult and schismatic dissidence such as Donatism, the
empire would become 'a Christian empire' (GC ii.18).
(This last phrase occurs only once in Augustine's
voluminous writings, but the thought is implicit in several
places and he liked to speak of 'the Christian world'.) If so,
it was not inherent in all government as such that it must
seek a monopoly of power and loyalty and try to annihilate
the Church as a threat to its own sovereignty. Moreover, St
Paul (Romans 13) had given authoritative support to a

positive evaluation of government as a providential instrument of order—if not getting one to heaven, at least hedging the road to hell.

The mature Augustine of the *City of God* no longer used such optimistic words about political structures. Constantine's conversion had been very welcome, but had not introduced the millennium. The nineteenth book analyses the overlap of values between the earthly and heavenly cities. Certainly they are utterly distinct, the secular from the sacred, Babylon from Jerusalem. The earthly city which is organized for power and wealth, comfort and pleasure, is poles apart from the heavenly city. The values of the city of God are sought even in this life by the Church which, to that degree, is identifiable (Matt. 13) with the kingdom of God. But though the difference is on a truly apocalyptic scale, nevertheless both cities are concerned with two things which they have in common, justice and peace, though by these words they do not always mean exactly the same things.

In regard to justice, the city of God had an obvious bias to the poor. Augustine noticed that the most vocal defenders of paganism were in general defenders of the old social order in which the poor fawned on the rich, and the rich exploited their dependent clients (CD 2.20). He realized how inadequate was private almsgiving and the Church chest with its register of paupers daily fed from the soup kitchen. The dimensions of destitution were too great to be met except by redistributive taxation (CD 5.17).

When a pagan intellectual contended that the Sermon on the Mount could not be put into practice without bringing the empire to an end, Augustine replied unabashed that retaliation for injuries was no way to make any society work, so that Christ's principles were far from irrelevant to the happiness and tranquillity of the secular world. An affluent society obsessed with wealth and power suffered the anxieties and all the diabolical pride and envy which haunted very rich individuals. With remarkable prescience

of what was to come in the West within a generation after
his death, Augustine suggested that the world would be a
happier place if the great and proud empire were succeeded
by a number of smaller states (CD iv.15). The kingdom of
God had as much room for Goths as for Romans.

Augustine's language angered imperialist patriots. He
was aware that empires come and go. He did not think the
Roman Empire was doomed, as some contemporary
pessimists were saying. Rome would collapse only if the
Romans did. People cursed the times they lived in; 'but
whether times are good or bad depends on the moral quality
of individual and social life, and is up to us' (S 80.8). Each
generation, he remarked, thinks its own times uniquely
awful (S 25); that morality and religion have never been at
so low an ebb as in their generation, and civilized values
have never been more threatened. He thought it his duty to
attack fatalism and to arouse people to a sense of being
responsible if things went wrong. They could have a say in
what was going to happen next.

Augustine did not define the 'peace', for which both
Church and Empire strove, in merely political or civil terms
as if it were merely the result of some fragile and transitory
compromise in the unending struggle for power. He granted
that only a strong government could assure people of peace
and enable them to live without fear of social disorder.
Roman law, which he knew quite a lot about, he treated
with deep respect as indispensable for the coherence of
society. One should not, for example, simply take the law
into one's own hands when confronted by a bandit. Law and
government are necessary because of the distortion, greed,
and anti-social corruption in the human heart. At the same
time this corruption goes so deep that there can be no true
peace without the healing grace of God. The foundation of
peace is a justice which gives each his due. True peace and
true justice lie beyond this world as it is and will be, and
belong to a higher order of God's purpose. Admittedly, the
number of citizens whose lives are touched by grace is not

more than a very substantial minority, but that minority can be of crucial importance. He well understood that government is more effective in suppressing vice than in stimulating virtue. Governors had a prime responsibility to provide for defence, public order, the physical comfort and prosperity, perhaps even the entertainment of the people. But it was not without a responsibility for civic virtue. If a proconsul or a magistrate were a Christian, then he had a religious and public duty to support goodness and truth and those concerned to disseminate them.

Augustine never wrote about political problems without an awareness that the system has to be established on the assumption that human cupidity will produce vast disorder unless there are restraints and penalties. Yet he still thought the world to belong to God; his world was not as ferocious as that of Thomas Hobbes, and he could speak of good government and legislation as dependent for its authority not on mere force, but on being recognized to possess a moral basis, and therefore a shadow or image of true justice, 'the eternal law'. Government was for him an exemplification of the providential principle of order imposed on the disruptive forces let loose by the Fall. In this respect order may not abolish what is wrong so much as adapt the evil to unintended and good purposes; e.g. slavery and private property.

The domination of one man over another may be abused, but it is the lesser of two evils where the alternative is anarchy and every man for himself. Augustine hated the slave trade. Whenever feasible, he used the church chest to emancipate slaves oppressed in bad households. On one occasion his people took direct action to liberate slaves from a ship in Hippo harbour, and the chest was used to reimburse the aggrieved owners. It was hard to stop destitute parents selling their children. Augustine was once nonplussed by a reasonably well-to-do tenant farmer who sold his wife and, when Augustine expostulated, declared that he preferred the money. Yet slavery was not an unmitigated evil when slaves in good homes were better clothed, fed, and housed than the free wage labourers who were the great majority of the labour force.

Order was so important that a malevolent if legitimate emperor had a right to obedience. The follower of Christ would render to Caesar the obedience of his body, and to God that of his mind and soul. Though 'like a traveller in a foreign land' (CD xix.17), his participation in political life, if qualified by his talents, should not be a passive acquiescence but a positive duty. Society needs people of integrity in the public service, as in commerce; people with the courage to withstand the Mafia-like bribery and threats of the powerful and rich. Augustine's remarks show that such people were rare.

For the Christian conscience, criminal justice and military service created the most problematic areas of moral decision. Augustine shared the almost universal view of the early Church that torture and capital punishment were unacceptable in a commonwealth informed by a Christian estimate of man. One must say 'almost universal' since there also existed an opinion, advocated by a solitary unnamed Christian jurist late in the fourth century, that the criminal code of the Christian empire should embody the retaliation principle of the Old Testament and be altogether stricter than traditional Roman law; in medieval times his little book became quite widely read. Augustine was much opposed to torture, which was regular in criminal procedure and especially treason trials; it made innocent people confess to acts they had not committed and left them maimed. Capital punishment he judged incompatible with a remedial intention; moreover, mistakes were sometimes made. On military service, however, he was less rigorous. He accepted that in self-defence or for the recovery of stolen property, force could be legitimate. Had not Cicero himself contended that wars should be fought only in self-defence or for upholding honour? For Augustine war was not a fitting way of settling disputes, and he shared the hope that in Christian times it might be checked. But he recognized that there would continue to be unjust aggression which had to be resisted for the sake of values that Christians held dear. When Sahara tribesmen attacked Roman settlements, he wrote to the Christian military commander exhorting him to consider it a religious duty to suppress the marauders.

Nevertheless Augustine believed it to be both a religious and a political necessity to maximize restraint in hostilities. The humanity demanded by religion was also politically correct. Wars, granted that they were sometimes necessary, must be conducted with such respect for humanity as to leave the opponent without the sense of being humiliated and resentful, thereby sowing the seeds of future conflict. Prisoners should never be killed (as was common in ancient warfare). If, however, a soldier found himself fighting in a war the justice of which seemed questionable, it was a sufficient acquittal of his conscience that he had to obey orders. But the general principles of the internal criminal code of a just empire were equally applicable to conflicts between States.

Like Plato and Aristotle, Augustine did not see the business of politics as divorced from all ethical issues, even though he did not think the secular world capable of establishing a truly just society.

In the *City of God* there are places where Rome is symbolic head of the earthly community in the grip of satanic forces, while the Church is at least an anticipation of God's city. The old apocalyptic antithesis is being given its full force, thereby creating the presuppositions of 'secularization' in the sense of the assumption that religion is a realm of concern irrelevant to the world's principal business of power, honour, wealth, and sex. But there are also texts where Rome is given a positive significance in God's purpose for his world, whereas the empirical Church is seen as failing to realize divine intentions because of compromises with the secular world. Augustine was certain that conversion to Christianity would alleviate some social and political problems but not provide instant solutions. The anti-Donatist writings show that he did not see 'Church and State' as independent powers. Although he believed a Christian ruler should support the Church and be known to be against sin, he would have been greatly astonished by the medieval canonists who interpreted him to imply that the empire ought to be run by bishops with the pope at their head. He passionately loved the Church, but the failures of its members, both clerical and lay, gave him moments of dark gloom.

At the conclusion of the *City of God* he came to state the Christian doctrine of the Last Things: the earthly and the heavenly city have their respective culminations in hell and heaven. The absoluteness of this black-and-white choice gave him misgivings. The Church on earth certainly included individuals of dedicated, if often inconspicuous, devotion and goodness, who realized the angelic condition in this life. It also included people whose conversion, at least initially, had had a very secular motivation: they feared annoying a powerful patron, or aspired to a lady's hand, or hoped it might bring them luck in commerce. Some came in quest of physical health, and Augustine was never slighting about those who did so, though the catechists should teach them that religion had higher ends. A majority of Augustine's church members were 'average sensual people'. On the foundation of faith, their moral record was more like combustible wood, hay, and stubble than gold or silver capable of surviving the purging fire of God's judgement (1 Cor. 3). They prayed God would forgive their faults and, for their hopes hereafter, they relied on God's mercy pleaded in the eucharistic memorial of Christ's redemption and on the intercession of the Church both living and departed. Augustine was never a man to suggest that the ethical demands on Christians are less than rigorous or that destiny hereafter is unrelated to conduct now; but he recognized that in the pilgrimage of the soul now and in the age to come the physical death of the body is but an incident along the road. In this life none is free of sin except Christ; and if, 'as piety demands', we add that Mary was free of actual sin (N 42), Augustine assumed that she was not born free of original sin, and is redeemed by her Son (P 34.3). Otherwise, the daily soiling of life in this world leaves everyone stained (CD xx.6.1).

Sanctification, therefore, was a long process which continued. After death there would be those whose 'sleep' would be disturbed by such dreams as would give them pause (S 328.5). 'Hell' Augustine thought not so much a physical place as a condition of the soul in blindness and alienation from God. Pagans mocked the notion as a bogy to frighten people into Church. But the Platonic philosophers themselves thought no sins pass unpunished, and that there is remedial correction and discipline. Augustine agreed that for all who so receive it divine punishment is remedial.

The *City of God* is treated incorrectly if it is regarded as a statement about political theory or as containing a philosophy of history intended to discern a divine pattern in the course of events. In fact, at many points in the work the argument is designed to show how hard it is to discern such a pattern. Great powers rise and fall in world history, and the reason why is anything but clear. The unpredictability both of death and of decisions by human wills means that much is uncertain. The believer holds that what is incoherent to the mind of man is coherent to God. Disasters may move one to tears, but should on no account provoke astonishment (E 111.2). Augustine offers much more hope to the individual than to the institutions of human society, peculiarly liable to be vehicles of group egotism. In any event, no Platonist could easily have a feeling for history in the sense of a self-sufficient, self-contained process with its own observable causes and effects and with goals that are immanent within the movement of causation.

10 Nature and grace

In his thirties, in reaction against Manicheism Augustine stressed both church authority and individual freedom. But even when writing on free choice he had declared that without God's grace to rescue fallen man, one cannot be set on the right path. This acknowledgement of weakness was not a disparagement of reason. Cicero's *Hortensius* always made him ask about the application of reason to the identification of happiness. In his maturity, aged sixty-six, he wrote a crushing rebuke to a self-taught and opinionated theologian who adopted a wholly fideist position and thought reason irrelevant to faith. 'Greatly cherish intellect', he told him (E 120.13 *intellectum valde ama*). Nevertheless, he was also sure that sin warps the judgement, weakens the will's determination. For sin impels the mind towards external things, away from the contemplation of transcendent realities. Hence the need for authority to implant the 'beginning of faith', which is then developed and consolidated by reason.

After Augustine had become a bishop, the theme of man's absolute need for grace rose to a crescendo. The anti-Manichee *Confessions* have at their heart a sense that sinful man, hamstrung by selfishness from the earliest moments of infancy, is the prisoner of habits which are second nature. Only grace can restore authentic freedom. Therefore, 'when God rewards our merits, he crowns his own gifts' (C ix.34—a formula he often repeated later, gratefully borrowed by the Council of Trent in 1547).

The *Confessions* became an immediate best-seller, which won Augustine many friends and gave critics additional grounds for being critical. Among the opulent aristocrats of Rome, now beginning to think it need not be un-Roman to turn to Christianity, the exquisite rhetoric was admired.

But the book was also taken to presuppose that moral compromises were pardonable. If, as Augustine repeatedly declared, continence could be had only as God's gift, could one not be tolerantly compassionate towards would-be believers who found such austere discipleship very costly?

At Rome by 400 there was a lay ascetic of British origin named Pelagius, popular as a spiritual counsellor in high society. After travels in the East he settled in Rome and wrote a commentary on St Paul's letters, partly designed to avert Manichee appeals to them. The east Christian theological tradition which helped to form Pelagius' mind was much more positive about human nature than was the Augustinian estimate. He feared both despair of human power to do what God commands, and also cheap grace. He felt it must be unthinkable that God would ever command the impossible. If man so chose, he had the power to keep the commandments, even that awkward one forbidding adultery. The substance of Christian worship lay in moral action rather than in the self-indulgent cultivation of mystical feelings. Did it not strike at the roots of endeavour if one held that from Adam each has inherited a flawed nature? To tell people that their will was corroded to the point of almost total incapacity seemed to Pelagius fatally enervating. No act could be counted as a sin unless deliberately chosen. Sin's universality Pelagius explained as the result of social habit after Adam had set a disastrous example. Certainly without the help of grace the sinner could not do all that he ought, and his duty is the imitation of Christ's example. But grace is assisting, not all-controlling. Oarsmen can get their craft to their destination without wind and sail, though sail makes it easier. There must be some moment when man actually resolves, really makes an effort, truly does something which is all his own. The doctrine that everything is the gift of grace, including the very will itself, seemed to Pelagius debilitating to the point of catastrophe.

The train of events which brought Augustine and

Pelagius into open controversy was very gradual. The two men were agreed on far more than that on which they disagreed. Both saw humanity as locked into a corporately sinful social tradition. Pelagius insisted that sin is not physically hereditary, and therefore by free choice one can escape. God (he said) had given moral laws for the conscience; free will; remission of sins in baptism and penance to rebuild resolve; above all, grace to help wherever there was truly good will. The grace of God would give illumination to know what was right, and extra assistance, short of doing absolutely everything. Augustine on the other hand was sure that if there was any point in the process of escape at which humanity was on its own, there egotism and perversity would take charge. For Pelagius sin and evil were a contingent, non-necessary fact. Augustine thought that, since the Fall, that had ceased to be the case, and pointed to the natural will's recoil from pure goodness and failure to take pleasure in it.

Both men saw the human condition as misery ending in death. Pelagius thought death a biological necessity. Augustine thought the fear of death could not be so universal or profound unless it were a penalty for sin.

Inherent in Augustine's lifelong concern to vindicate providence was his belief that no pain or loss is undeserved. This axiom, if applied with Pelagius in wholly individualist terms, must end by seeming to make God an arbitrary tyrant; or why are some people deformed or otherwise defective, often from birth? Augustine could never accept that inference. Therefore (he said) to be a member of the 'mass of perdition' it was enough to be one of Adam's posterity, as such excluded from access to bliss except by the merciful but inexplicable intervention of grace. Those who receive mercy can only be grateful for grace they had done nothing to deserve. Those who do not receive mercy can have no ground to complain of a justice which all in Adam deserve. Even they can bless God for the natural delights of this life. Though it is never said that the

109

non-elect are predestinated to damnation, Augustine was inclined to distinguish his view from Manichee dualism by stressing freedom in God, not freedom in man (DP 19). God allowed but had not actually decreed the loss of the reprobate.

He thought it self-evident that human nature as now constituted could not be normal, could not be as the Creator originally intended. Before the Fall man had the power by free choice not to sin, and no weakness of will hindered him from doing what was good. Had he not sinned, Adam would have lived with Eve for ever in immortality. But even in paradise Adam needed grace (CD xiv.27), not only as a helpful adjunct to his will but as an indispensable means. In his early exposition of Genesis in refutation of the Manichees, Augustine once explained in passing the two accounts of the creation of man, suggesting that the ensouled man may have received a divine inbreathing to raise his soul to the level of spirit. That would imply that supernatural grace was an addition to natural humanity even in paradise, and that this was what was lost at the Fall.

Pelagius seemed to Augustine to be advocating a half-Stoic humanism, asserting splendid ideals but quite failing to penetrate the abyss of the human heart. Moreover, though Pelagius had no such intention, his language was heard by Augustine to imply that for redemption the human example of Jesus is sufficient, and indeed that the sacraments of the Church may not really be necessary. But Augustine replied that Christians hastened to bring their infants to baptism for the remission of sins. The universal practice of infant baptism required no defence at all on an Augustinian view; it was the supreme illustration of the sovereignty of God's electing grace prior to any movement on the part of the individual's will, in no sense a reward for virtuous aspiration or action.

The question at issue in this last exchange of argument brings out the major point that Augustine's doctrine of the corruption of man's moral being required a balancing emphasis on the power and necessity of the objective means of grace ministered in the sacraments of the Church. Grace had its focus in the remission of sins pledged and communicated through baptism, and in the new life renewed in the eucharist. The implications for the authority of the Church were considerable.

When writing on free choice before he became a bishop, Augustine had speculated that infants dying unbaptized would find their destiny in neither heaven nor hell. The Pelagians accused the older Augustine of abandoning this wise suggestion, and of believing that a merciful and just God was capable of consigning babies to hell when their parents failed to get them to the font in time. Augustine agreed that such events were painful, but they were neither fate nor chance because in God's world nothing is (DP 31). From John 3 he felt certain that no one deliberately refusing baptism could get to heaven. If unbaptized babies are condemned, that was not because of any personal choice, but only because Adam's posterity shared in a collective alienation. The admitted necessity of baptism proved original sin, and the flaw in human nature proved the necessity of faith and baptism. It is clear that Augustine's view fused biological ideas of heredity with the idea of the juridical liability of humanity. He quickly found that he had sailed into a storm.

The Pelagian controversy drove him to occupy positions which critics, at the time and later, felt to be regrettable.

Among Augustine's critics the Pelagian Julian, bishop of Eclanum (near Benevento in south Italy), stands out as having a stature within range of Augustine's own. African pessimism was not, he felt, the natural air of the Italian churches. The last years of Augustine's life were devoted to sharp exchanges with him, in which fair comment was mingled with vulgar abuse. Julian picked on Augustine's language about the role of sexuality in the transmission of sinfulness. To Julian Augustine seemed to stand revealed as an impenitent Manichee, more influenced than he himself

111

realized by his decade under Mani's spell, hating the Creator's handiwork, and denying that in giving man free will God 'emancipated' humanity to stand on its own feet.

Augustine defended himself with intensity. He was vindicated, he felt, by the way in which all human beings regard sex as a source of personal and social difficulty. In animals the mating instinct operates only at certain times of the year; in man the impulse puts him continually in trouble (S Frangip. i.8). Shame is a universal phenomenon. Within marriage itself, where sexual union is honourable beyond question, the act normally takes place in privacy and darkness. Cynic philosophers so outraged public opinion by copulating in the streets that they had long stopped doing that by Augustine's time. Outside marriage sex attracted fascinated gossip. The gulf between dignity and animality made the subject central to much comedy. Why are tabu words coined except to express humanity's combination of fascination and revulsion? Town brothels are in special areas, not the main street. There is an intuitive sense that sexuality can come into tension with higher aspirations.

Augustine repeatedly made capital out of an argument that seems bizarre to the modern reader. The physiological changes that make sexual union practicable are uncontrolled by reason or will. Body and reason can often be at loggerheads, the body stirred when the will and reason do not want it, or vice versa. Moreover, 'sexual ecstasy swamps the mind', obliterating rational thought (J 4.7). In this irrational and involuntary character of the impulse Augustine saw the ultimate demonstration of the truth of his view. He did not understand anything about reflexes. He therefore constructed an imaginative picture of the sex-life of Adam and Eve before the Fall (if indeed the Fall did not occur very soon after the creation of Eve). Their union must have been tranquil and under the control of the will, just as we can move our hands and feet whenever we wish. Their union in paradise was a source of 'supreme pleasure'. Augustine did not accept the old notions, popular among gnostic sects of the second century, that the Fall consisted in the serpent's seduction of Eve or that Adam and Eve fell by having sexual union before the proper time. He vehemently disavowed the view (which he had once held) that sexual intercourse was a result of the Fall. But the Fall had affected it.

His considerable discussions of sexuality are conspicuously free from prudery, so frank that he feared being read by people whose minds were unequal to the seriousness of the subject. Medicine was a department of science on which he made himself informed. His library included clinical textbooks and, while composing his replies to Julian of Eclanum, he studied the best guide to gynaecology. In any event, no one could accuse him of being a remote celibate who did not know what he was talking about. As a bishop he felt he had a duty and a right to tell married Christians what they might or, in Lent, might not do in bed.

As we have seen, his estimate of sexuality was marked by tension between his personal renunciation and a positive Catholic evaluation of the beauty of bodily form given by the Creator (e.g. R ii.15). But the most positive estimate could not eliminate the truth of experience that even for married couples sex can have its problems. The body can be disobedient to both will and reason, and (adopting an idea from Porphyry) Augustine saw that fact as a penalty for the soul's resistance to the divine goodness. So the physical act was, he urged, the vehicle for the transmission of the flawed human nature subsequent to the Fall. Were that not the case, the New Testament would not have regarded married life as surpassed by the greater good of celibacy—again a view shared by Porphyry. Hence 'the very root of sin lies in carnal generation' (PM ii.15).

Augustine boldly suggested that this hypothesis explained why Jesus was born of a Virgin (a miracle which, like the Resurrection, evoked much pagan criticism): from Mary Jesus took 'the likeness of sinful flesh' (St Paul's phrase), not a flesh flawed by original sin. Thereby Augustine injected a powerful and toxic theme into medieval theology, namely that the Virgin Birth presupposes that even within marriage the sexual act cannot be done without some taint of cupidity. In the twelfth century the presuppositions latent in this view were exposed and vigorously attacked by Peter Abelard and Robert of Melun.

Nevertheless, Augustine was aware that he needed to safeguard his ascetic stance against overstatement. When about 390 a critic of asceticism named Jovinian (himself a monk) denied that virginity as such is morally superior to marriage, Jerome's onslaught upon him became such a hymn of hate against sex and marriage that the charges of Manicheism came to look uncommonly plausible. To avert the consequence of Jerome's grosser indiscretions, Augustine wrote in 401 a treatise *On the Good of Marriage*. The book was addressed to nuns warning them that, while they had indeed chosen a higher life, they must not disparage Christian marriage. The physical delight inevitably accompanying the sexual act ought to be distinguished from the libido which is a wrong use of the impulse. He defined three good constituents of marriage in terms which did not include mutual delight. They were procreation, mutual fidelity, and the 'sacrament' or rule of indissolubility (i.e. the ban on remarriage after divorce or separation). This last point of indissolubility was one concerning which, in the light of Matt. 5: 32 and 1 Cor. 7: 10–11, he long felt hesitations, gradually moving to a strict and rigorist position in the later stages of the Pelagian controversy.

Marriage, Augustine taught, was constituted by the consent of the couple rather than by physical consummation. (He accepted the view dominant in Roman law.) And while the sexual act was primarily intended for procreation, Augustine judged it 'pardonable' if married people enjoyed conjugal union without the intention to procreate. Like Aristotle and St Paul, he laid stress on the mutual obligations of the partners (above, p. 89). He recommended the maximum restraint to serious and highminded Christian couples, and thought nothing more beautiful than the sexless friendship of the elderly. But he readily conceded, indeed insisted, that in Christian marriage the carnal impulse is put to 'a good and right use'. What he could not bring himself to say is that what is being used is in itself morally indifferent or a most natural act for the divinely created animal nature of man. But then the Platonic tradition made him want to define the essence of man in terms which almost omitted the physical nature of the creature. He could cite Aristotle's familiar definition of man as a rational mortal animal, but certainly preferred to speak of man as a soul united to a body, or using a body.

Another major point at which controversy impelled Augustine into the use of tougher language than many found congenial was the doctrine of predestination with the related question of perseverance, subjects felt to be so complex that eleven centuries later the Council of Trent wore kid gloves to deal with them and gave verdicts which removed none of the serious ambiguities. (Thereby it opened the door to the Jansenist controversy.) Augustine understood the priority of grace to entail the conclusion that God could not finally allow his elect to fall away from grace. Predestination must imply that the intended destination would be reached. So while human foreknowledge is not causative, God's foreknowledge is. Augustine could not abide the notion, found almost universally in the Greek theologians of his age, that the divine decree of predestination is based on foreseen merits. Nothing in man, past, present, or future, can be the moving or meritorious cause of God's election. The acute difficulty, that this treats God as a wholly inscrutable arbitrary autocrat, Augustine had to meet with his dictum that God not only predestinates but also imparts merits. And he saw in Jesus himself the best illustration of his point. As being one with God, his goodness could not be contingent or in any sense precarious. He could not sin, we can. But if we are among the elect, surely we shall rise from sin to fulfil God's predetermined purpose. 'The whole Christ' (above, p. 84) is predestinate.

Augustine granted, indeed insisted, that the elect can never know for certain whether or not they are elect, unless it be most exceptionally by private revelation. There could be only one empirical test of election, and that a necessary but not a sufficient test, namely perseverance to one's last breath, dying in a state of grace. But God alone knows who are his own. Perseverance is an unmerited gift of grace, just as is also the initial turning of the will to God in faith and penitence.

Augustine's doctrines elicited vehement criticism among monks in North Africa and most notably in Southern Gaul at Marseille and Lérins. From Aquitaine he received staunch support. (Over many centuries a high proportion of the controversies about the Augustinian doctrine of predestination have taken place on French soil.)

Augustine's critics fastened on the evident fact that his doctrine of predestination appealed to a partial selection of texts in scripture and had to use force on other texts which did not fit his thesis. The New Testament text that 'God wills all to be saved' had to be interpreted to mean that the elect include representatives of every race of mankind (CG 44). The critics' case against him is almost reducible to the weighty charge that he had (inconsistently) strayed into 'curiosity'—claiming to inquire into matters God has not revealed and which lie beyond human knowledge. But behind the anxieties there was the reasonable apprehension that the Augustinian doctrine would produce moral carelessness. Many of his critics in southern Gaul supported his opposition to Pelagius and Julian, but were embarrassed by the arguments he deployed.

From time to time high Augustinian doctrines of election have been advocated in Christian history, as by Gottschalk in the ninth century, by John Calvin in the sixteenth, by

Jansenius in the seventeenth. They have invariably provoked opposition which has sought to avoid the Pelagian alternative, but at the same time to preserve the freedom of the will and human responsibility. Augustine's own verdict on the discussion of grace and free will in a book he wrote for Simplicianus of Milan (above, p. 16) may stand for a summary of the problem as his opponents, themselves anti-Pelagian too, saw the matter: 'In trying to solve this question I made strenuous efforts on behalf of the preservation of the free choice of the human will, but the grace of God defeated me' (R ii.1).

Augustine came to enjoy far-reaching influence during his lifetime as a result of his writings, which circulated wherever Latin was read. Correspondents unknown to him used to write asking him to unravel their puzzles or hoping (usually vainly) that he would smile on their own theological efforts. Even Jerome during the last year of his life sent a most flattering letter from Bethlehem to tell him that by his books he had virtually 'refounded the old faith', and that the bitter attacks on him by heretics were sufficient testimony to his achievement (E 195). Augustine himself was never less than embarrassed to be treated as an 'authority' in the sense of not being expected to give reasons. Only holy scripture and, where that was silent or ambiguous, ecumenical consensus had such authority for believers. Moreover, his ideal was to continue correcting and improving his understanding to his dying day. In general he was not a man out to defend a position merely because he had himself once adopted it. His method with his critics was often to point out the difficulties in their position and to suggest that he preferred to live with his own. His work always reflected the critical independence of his mind, and perhaps his supreme forte was a rare ability to get to the heart of a complicated question. Without being a technical philosopher in a professional sense, his mind was well equipped, and his writing remains of considerable interest to the philosophically-minded concerned with the Platonic tradition. Much of Plotinus got into his bloodstream, but he remained pre-eminently a master of persuasive speech. Despite his conversion from rhetoric to philosophy in 386, the effect of ordination five years afterwards was to put him back into a situation where oratory again became important to him, with the fresh conviction that he was advocate not of some human interest but of the very truth of God. A fascination with words never left him.

Edward Gibbon scornfully wrote of Augustine: 'His learning is too often borrowed and his arguments are too often his own.' A modern scholar would take out the scorn and invert the judgement. His learning was largely his own. He always had a fine library to hand, both in classical and in Christian literature (including Greek theologians), and his mind was richly stocked with classical literature. He knew how to use his books. As for his arguments, many are in fact often borrowed, especially from Porphyry and Cicero, whose *Hortensius* he could never forget. The borrowing from the Neoplatonists did not mean that his debt was not coupled with critical dissent.

Gibbon's scorn articulated the general hostility towards Augustinianism characteristic of the eighteenth-century Enlightenment. For that hostility there were reasons. The bitter wrangles of the Reformation and Counter-Reformation, producing long wars that inflicted vast damage, had largely been disputes between different interpretations of Augustine's doctrine of the Church and of grace. The sixteenth century controversy about justification by grace alone on condition of faith alone (a controversy which seemed boring and irrelevant to the eighteenth-century men of reason) was conducted within an Augustinian and medieval framework of ideas, and was a further chapter in the dispute about the relation between nature and grace. In the sixteenth century both sides made great appeal to Augustine. The Council of Trent's decree on justification (1547) was a mosaic of Augustinian phrases, so anti-

Pelagian that the Protestants could not bring themselves to believe in its sincerity. Above all, the Augustinian denial of human capacity for perfectibility had, especially among Jansenists and Calvinists, representatives against whom the Enlightenment was in sharp reaction.

Again, Augustine stood for the ascetic ideal. The Protestant Reformation enlisted widespread lay support by its politically motivated aversion to the monastic ideal, which lay anticlericals opposed as absorbing too much wealth in support of its institutions. Although there is no fundamental tension between ascetic discipline in community and the doctrine of justification by grace on condition of faith, Luther had tried to argue that monastic vows are inconsistent with New Testament Christianity. The Enlightenment shared the aversion, but accepted the Counter-Reformation's Augustinian conviction that ascetic renunciation of natural goods was taught in the New Testament. Voltaire and Gibbon saw this inherent asceticism of Christianity as a ground for rejecting it: the gospel of grace and peace did nothing to make the world materially richer, and discouraged military grandeur.

Augustine certainly thought authentic Christianity otherworldly. It derived its reference-points and criteria from considerations beyond the process of time and history. Though convinced that this world is God's world, he did not believe that human life can belong wholly to the secular and material order, or that the primary values can be power, honour, wealth and sex. Cicero had indelibly printed on his mind that they can be no road to happiness, either for the individual or for society.

Short reading list

The edition of Augustine by the Benedictines of St Maur (Paris, 1679–1700), often reprinted, is in J. P. Migne, *Patrologia Latina* (Paris, 1841–2). Further sermons in G. Morin, *Sermones post Maurinos reperti* (Rome, 1930) and C. Lambot, *Sermones Selecti* (Utrecht, 1950). A guide to these in P. P. Verbraken, *Études critiques sur les sermons authentiques de S. Augustin* (Steenbrugge, 1976).

Many principal works have modern editions in the two series, Corpus Scriptorum Ecclesiasticorum Latinorum and Corpus Christianorum.

For a high proportion English translations exist, such as in the Oxford Library of the Fathers (1838–81), a series edited by M. Dods (T. & T. Clark, and Eerdmans), and three recent series, Library of Christian Classics, Fathers of the Church, and Ancient Christian Writers. Penguin translations of *Confessions* (R. Pine-Coffin, London, 1961) and *The City of God* (H. Bettenson, London, 1972, new ed. 1984). The best edition of the *Confessions* is by A. Solignac (Paris, 1962).

For biography without the theology see the excellent Life by Peter Brown (London, 1967). On the ideas see E. Gilson, *The Philosophy of St Augustine* (Eng. tr., London, 1960); J. Burnaby, *Amor Dei* (London, 1938); G. Bonner, *Augustine, Life and Controversies* (London, 1964, new ed. Norwich, 1986); E. TeSelle, *Augustine the Theologian* (New York, 1970); R. A. Markus (ed.), *Augustine: A Collection of Critical Essays* (New York, 1972); on the Church, R. F. Evans, *One and Holy* (London, 1972); on ethics, H. A. Deane, *The Political and Social Ideas of St Augustine* (Columbia, paperback 1963). On the Donatist schism: W. H. C. Frend, *The Donatist Church* (Oxford, 1952, reprinted 1985). Neoplatonism: J. J. O'Meara, *The Young Augustine* (London, 1954, paperback 1980); G. R. Evans, *Augustine on Evil* (Cambridge, 1982); R. Sorabji, *Time, Creation and the Continuum* (London, 1983); Paul Henry, *The Path to Transcendence* (Eng. tr. Pittsburgh, 1981); P. Courcelle, *Late Latin Writers and their Greek Sources* (Eng. tr., Harvard, 1969). H. Hagendahl, *Augustine and the Latin Classics* (Gothenburg, 1967).

Plotinus is edited and translated by A. H. Armstrong, Loeb Classical Library. An annual survey of literature on Augustine appears in *Revue des études augustiniennes* (Paris).

Index